Wild Pivot

Wild Pivot

NOTES FROM A POLITICAL LIFE REWRITTEN

Jen Thompson

SWP
SHE WRITES PRESS

Published in 2026 by
She Writes Press, an imprint of The Stable Book Group

SWP

1569 Solano Ave #546
Berkeley, CA 94707
https://shewritespress.com

Library of Congress Control Number: 2026909458
ISBN: 979-8-89636-146-6
eISBN: 979-8-89636-147-3

Interior designer: Katherine Lloyd, The DESK

Printed in the United States

Names and identifying characteristics have been changed to protect the privacy of certain individuals.

To Jack and Michael

May you always be known and treasured
just as you are.

Let no man deceive himself.
If any man among you seemeth to be wise in this world,
let him become a fool, that he may be wise.
I Corinthians 3:18

Prologue

THE ROYAL BOTANICAL GARDENS

February 14, 2003 (Age 31)

Grant's striking blue eyes watched as I stretched myself across the red-and-black checkered wool blanket. Blankets like ours circled the grassy, open field like lily pads, with wicker baskets of wine anchoring them in place. Tall oaks and leafy plants edged the park. Tonight's Moonlight Cinema show began at twilight, when the azure Australian sky gave way to darkness and the Melbourne skyline lit up in the distance. Wine glasses clinked and people laughed, but when *Breakfast at Tiffany's* began flashing across the massive outdoor screen, the field became quiet. Grant leaned over to kiss me, exactly as I'd hoped he would, and I laced my fingers through the strands of his lovely brown hair while his hands pressed my body into his chest. At thirty-one, I was old enough to know better than to jump into bed with gorgeous men like Grant, men who had foreign accents and eyes the color of the sea, just so that I could dull the pain of my memories. But being old enough to know better and experienced enough to act that way were two very different things.

To put the truth of my situation mildly, it had been a rough year. I'd come through hell working around the clock to win a

Senate campaign for my congressman boss, and those grueling months had taken a severe toll. I had been sued and slandered on the front pages of newspapers, I had been cheated on and lied to, and I'd suffered a horrific accident that nearly killed me. By Election Day, I knew I had to escape, and Australia was the farthest place I could think to go. When the University of Melbourne offered me a visiting professorship, a university office, and a place to live after the campaign ended, I took it.

After fifteen punishing months on the campaign trail, I could almost hear the giant sucking sound when I landed in Australia in early December. I didn't know one person on the entire continent, and with several weeks to go until my professorship officially started, my world instantly became silent and insular. When the crushing intensity of my political life suddenly ended, a deep, hollow void rushed in. Silence pressed in on me. I was not prepared for the overwhelming force of my thoughts, which I'd ignored for years, finally having their day in the sun. My confusing memories and questions about what I believed overtook me and brought me to my knees.

I knew it was crazy to be here. When we won the campaign, job offers poured in to work as a chief of staff in the Senate and as a political adviser in the White House, and I became a minor celebrity in Republican political circles. When I turned all of them down to take an unpaid visiting professorship in Australia, my colleagues were in apoplectic disbelief. For a decade, I'd worked eighty-hour weeks to climb into the seat of power I now claimed, and when I walked away, they thought I'd lost my marbles. Making it even worse, my colleagues joked about my embarrassingly old age of thirty-one for a "finding myself" journey, especially at the height of my career. One of my closest friends (who also happened to be President Bush's godson) remarked that he'd been nineteen when he'd made a similar expedition to Australia. The unavoidable problem that I couldn't talk about with my Republican friends (which was *all* of my friends), for fear of complete abandonment, was that I'd recently discovered I was a fraud. By the end of the campaign, I'd seen with a laser clarity that the woman I'd carefully created myself to be was not me at all, and I did not authentically believe anything I'd stood for in campaign politics. It was a realization that rocked me to my core.

Landing in Australia on that rainy, early-December morning was one of the most freeing moments of my life. It was also the most terrifying. Where was I supposed to begin?

Into my life's void—and a Melbourne pub called The Elephant and Wheelbarrow—walked handsome, sexy Grant with his ocean-blue eyes, a financial wizard by day at a large investment bank in Melbourne, an ocean lifeguard (with matching body) on the weekends, and a man whose touch melted me. Now, two months later, on Valentine's Day, at the Royal Botanical Gardens beneath the magnificent stars of the Southern Hemisphere, I longed to have Grant distract me from thinking about my past. I tried to focus my attention on the touch of his fingers lingering on my bare stomach and the sweetness of the Malbec on his breath. But my brain was not getting the memo. My mind, of its own volition, kept launching me back in time—four months, then eight months, then a year. How had I missed so many warning signs for so long?

I laid my head on the wool blanket and looked up at the sky. I never got used to the large, grey-headed flying foxes that glided through the air between the trees in Melbourne. From below, they looked like winged chihuahuas being shot from cannons.

"Do you have them in America?" Grant asked. He was watching the flying foxes, too.

"No," I said. "We only have regular bats. Everything is so different here."

Grant became used to me drifting off to places he could not go. He never pressed me for details, always intent on steering clear of my melancholy. Grant was far too handsome to be overly interested in anything long-term with a moody American who had too much time on her hands.

I needed to begin making peace with myself and my past. Moving to Australia had been the first step, and the easiest. But like all uncomfortable truths, I knew I could only achieve peace proportionate to my willingness to uncover my own secrets. I kept returning to the memory of standing on the ballroom stage next to my boss, the senator-elect from Missouri, as TV cameras livestreamed our image around the world only three months ago. We were on the winner's podium due, in great part, to my work. The United States Senate had been returned to Republican control. As the cameras flashed, I kept thinking, *My God, what have I done?* I could not get off that stage fast enough, and I left St. Louis two days later.

Many other memories from the past year also flashed through my mind like snapshots: divorcing my husband, being sued, having horrible newspaper articles written about me, getting in a debilitating car accident. I knew it was time to begin the search to understand how all these things had happened to me. But I was afraid.

Watching me stir, Grant asked, "Are you ready to go?"

I paused. "No. It's peaceful here. Let's stay awhile longer."

Grant poured another glass of Malbec for me, and I looked at his face. No man, not even one as beautiful as Grant, could save me from my confusion about what was happening to me. Nor could living in a magical place as far away from my home as Australia. Geography, after all, was just geography. The search for light and inspiration needed to begin from inside my own skin and soul. I wondered how long it would take to find them. A few months? Maybe a year?

I leaned back into Grant, wanting to feel the warmth of his embrace. I kissed him with a long, slow kiss. My quest to understand my past would need to wait at least a few more hours. When I pulled my lips away from his, we rested on our sides and sipped our wine while Holly Golightly sang "Moon River" from the fire escape of her New York apartment, her voice reaching far beyond the open field.

WHAT I KNOW TO BE TRUE

December 2023 (Age 52)

Twenty-one years after my night with Grant at the Moonlight Cinema, I sat under a large oak tree on the college campus where I worked and let a news headline sink in: "Meet the Players at the Center of the Supreme Court's New Trump Drama." I read the article four times before putting my phone down next to me. For twenty years, I'd moved across the earth and back again to escape my past. I had come to the realization that I never would.

In front of me, green grass pushed up between the stones on the ground of the university's Greek Theatre, and sky-high palm trees swayed when the wind blew, their fronds rustling gently. The oaks were distinctive in Southern California's dry desert soil, and they grounded the landscape. Peace lived in this place. But news stories like this one catapulted me back to my political days in Washington, DC, when I'd worked inside the gray stone buildings on Capitol Hill, which were filled with the impressive offices of some of the nation's greatest minds and dullest men.

This time, the breaking news was that the thirty-year-old son of the Republican politician I'd worked to elect to the United

States Senate two decades ago was one of three attorneys of record representing former President Trump. Now a brilliant Stanford-educated lawyer, in my mind's eye, he was still a ten-year-old boy with messy brown hair and dirty jeans. I'd eaten dinner at his family's house twice every week while managing his father's campaign, and Uno was always our game of choice. Sometimes we'd head into their backyard, where I pushed him and his younger sisters on the swings. They'd nicknamed me Miss Blueberry because they thought blueberries were my favorite food.

"Miss Blueberry!" he and his sisters would yell. "Push me higher!" I'd step back several feet and pretend to gather momentum before rushing forward and giving them a giant heave into the air. They always squealed in delight. "Yaaaaayyyy Missss Bluuuuuueberrrryyyy!"

They didn't know it, but in those months, stress and anxiety forced me to eat only Luna Bars and blueberries, and I only drank Diet Coke. Nor could they have guessed that my pants accidentally fell to my ankles so often because I'd lost forty pounds in three months.

Discovering news connections to my past became a common occurrence. My younger years were braided with recent political events that had nothing to do with me yet held me captive inside them. Just a few weeks before seeing the Supreme Court headline, I'd read that a former close colleague was running Trump's 2024 presidential campaign as his closest ally. Before that, news that a political friend from Missouri had become the right-hand man to Governor Ron DeSantis, and Senator Cruz before him. In my most vivid memory of this friend, we danced together on the tabletops at a dive bar in Kansas City to Eminem's "Lose Yourself" while smoking Robusto cigars. A youngster I had hired straight out of Florida State University to work on the 2002 campaign had most recently been the political director for Kanye West.

Prologue

For years, I carried doubts about whether I was the woman in my memories. I channeled the sensation of being a performer in a circus sideshow act; there was me, and then there was the woman who had tragically snapped her whip at the lions and bears onstage, so politically incorrect and horrifying that I could not look away.

Who the hell was the woman in those memories, anyway?

Three years ago, when I'd started seeing a therapist for the first time, she'd asked me what I remembered from those days. Diving into my memories felt like opening a door to a heavily guarded room while mental spears whizzed by, protecting my past from my own self. Every time I recalled something, my body responded with an ache.

"Where do you feel it?" my therapist asked.

I pressed hard on my chest. "Here," I said, feeling my ribcage and breathing in the pain like she'd taught me. "Right here."

I exhaled.

She typed something into her computer, and I pondered my confusion.

"There is something wrong with me," I told her.

"Why do you say that?"

"Because look at my life. I have made it so difficult for myself. What if I hadn't turned down those job offers to be a chief of staff in the Senate or to work in the White House? What if I hadn't abandoned my perfect life? Things would be so easy now. My focus would be clear. That's how it is for all my former political friends."

She paused for a long time, but she did not look away.

"Would you go back and change your decision if you could?"

I did not need time to think. I knew the answer, and it felt good to say it out loud.

"No damn way."

"Well, Jen, there you go."

No. Damn. Way.

CHASING THE BOAR

May 2024 (Age 52)

On a recent afternoon, I scribbled down an old proverb I'd memorized long ago and taped it to the side of my computer: *Discovering the meaning of our lives, or God, is like chasing a wild boar through the forest. Even if you search for many days, you might never catch the boar; you might not even catch a glimpse of him. But there is no chance of catching the boar if you don't attempt the chase.*

People who know me now are shocked to learn about my past. They always ask the same question: How is it possible for a person to change so fundamentally?

In an era where quick fixes and easy buttons seem to be the only tenable solutions, my honest answer is unsatisfying. For many years, I walked through hellfire to make peace with my past, and I've been burned and charred into someone new along the way. My journey has taken a very long time. *Is* taking a long time. Indeed, I am still walking.

I would like to think my transformation provides some measure of hope. From my younger years to now, my politics, religion, understanding of women's rights, and ideas about racial and social justice have changed, just as I have changed. In a divided, vitriolic society where we cling to our blindness and we rarely change our minds about ourselves and our relationships with other human beings, the question is often asked: But what if we could be changed?

For my own part, I remain chasing the boar.

Part One

Wired

CHAPTER 1

Time Bomb: Five. Four. Three. Two. One. Boom.

SCENE ONE: COMING UNDONE

Spring 2012 (Age 40)

The TV cameraman set up his tripod for the live shot on the plaza steps while I sat next to him, studying my notes. The warm afternoon air carried the green pollen dust of springtime, and I sneezed before looking up. The white WRIC News–Richmond van was wedged between cars parked on Main Street. Behind it, traffic honked its way toward the old cobblestone streets and historic gas lanterns of Shockoe Bottom.

The biggest interview of my career as a part-time political commentator was about to begin. My mind raced. I could not focus. My eyes—and my attention—bounced from car to car, from building to building, and from my notes to the TV camera. I cupped my hand over my mouth and breathed into it. *Huhhhh*. I couldn't detect the smell of vodka, but then again, I never could.

A lone bird tweeted, and I spotted her, small, brown and white, about twenty feet away. She sat on a spindly branch in a small crepe myrtle tree that had been unnaturally planted between concrete pavers to provide shade. My eyes darted skyward and I craned my neck. A tall building towered above. It housed lawyers, like me.

A car pulled up next to the TV van, and Senator George Allen stepped out of the back seat. A handsome, distinguished-looking man, Senator Allen had served as a Republican senator and a Virginia governor before that. He'd lost a close election and was mounting a new campaign to reclaim his Senate seat. I walked over to him.

"Hello, Senator!"

"Hi, Jen. How are you? It's good to see you."

We knew one another. Senator Allen had been the chair of the National Republican Senatorial Committee when I ran Congressman Jim Talent's Senate campaign in 2002.

"How nice it is to be interviewed by an actual friend—a Republican—for a change," he joked.

Is that what I am? I wondered. For as often as I questioned which political party I now belonged to, I could never seem to arrive at a sufficient answer. I secretly hated Republicans almost as much as I hated Democrats.

"Senator, I'm going to ask you questions you've not been asked before." I said this with great conviction, as if I were Barbara Walters and not a part-time local political commentator.

He looked at me quizzically and with concern. I have no idea why I said what I did, nor do I know what happened next. The four vodka and Diet Cokes I'd quickly swallowed before arriving on the plaza kicked into my bloodstream with a force so overwhelming that I couldn't recollect anything I'd wanted to ask. I looked at my notes, but confusion muddied my brain.

Time Bomb: Five. Four. Three. Two. One. Boom.

I thought I was back on the campaign trail in Missouri even though it was ten years later and Senator Allen and I stood on a plaza in downtown Richmond, Virginia, on a warm spring afternoon.

At some point, I must have wrapped up our interview and left because I found myself at a restaurant in downtown Richmond—although I don't remember doing either. The next thing I remember is looking up at Winston Churchill, who was staring down at me from the top shelf of the bar. This Winston was a cement bust, the inexpensive kind sold on Amazon. Even so, his etched, vacant eyes looked straight through me, and his plaster of paris cigar hung judgingly from his mouth. *Cometh the hour, cometh the man* was the Churchill line I knew best, and here I obediently was—6:00 p.m. and my butt was firmly planted on the barstool.

The restaurant owner, Paul, stood across from me, wiping a pint glass with a towel.

"So, how did the interview go?" he asked.

"It went fine, I guess," I replied.

"What did you ask him?"

"I honestly can't remember," I said, and I couldn't. That was when my cell phone started ringing. From the caller ID, I saw it was Juan, the most popular TV news anchorman in the Richmond metro region and the man whose idea it had been for me to interview Senator Allen.

I picked up the phone and spoke before Juan could. Going on the offensive had always been my forte, a strategy that usually worked when I was sober, which I wasn't.

"Pretty good interview, eh, Juan?"

"Oh, Jen. What were you thinking?" His disappointment hung on each word.

"What do you mean?" I pretended I didn't know.

"Were you drunk?"

"Of course not!" I said at the same moment I realized I was slurring. I sat up straighter on my stool to appear composed.

There was silence. Without thinking, I picked up my cocktail. The ice rattled.

"Shit!" I said under my breath. I steadied the glass before taking a sip.

"Where are you?"

"At the restaurant. Do you want to meet me for dinner?"

"You should go home, Jen."

I moved my mouth to respond, "Don't be ridiculous!" but I couldn't properly conjure the "d" sound. I think I said a word that sounded like "reekickyoulus."

His silent disdain poured through the phone.

"I'll talk to you later."

"All right, Juan."

I heard him hang up. Even in my drunkenness, I knew I'd screwed up. Again.

"Everything okay?" Paul still stood in front of me, drying what looked like the same glass as before.

"Juan is pissed off at me."

I looked at my phone again and wished I was dead. I ordered another drink.

SCENE TWO: GHOSTS

June 2005 (Age 33)

At 1:30 p.m. on a Tuesday afternoon, I was sitting on the top step of a long-abandoned bank building in Richmond. The building looked like it was straight out of the *Mary Poppins* movie set with its stone columns and blackened windows. The only thing missing was Julie Andrews singing and feeding the birds.

Time Bomb: Five. Four. Three. Two. One. Boom.

People stared at me as they walked by on the sidewalk, like gawkers at a car accident. As soon as our eyes connected, they quickly looked away. Embarrassment crossed their faces. At the top of the steps, I was crying giant, heaving sobs that I could not control.

It was exactly two years, six months, and nine days after Election Night in 2002 when TV stations across the world had projected my image as a woman of immense power. Wearing a $1,500 suit and Prada boots I'd bought at Neiman Marcus that morning, I stood on the hotel ballroom stage next to my boss, Republican Senator-elect Jim Talent, while congratulatory calls and emails poured in from the White House, Capitol Hill, and every corner of the political spectrum.

Now, I had no money to my name, no permanent job, and no hope. I wore a blue-and-white seersucker dress from Target that stuck to my body in the heat, and my feet were sliding around in my inexpensive white sandals.

Richmond is an old city, the capital of the Confederacy during the Civil War. It was burned to the ground by Northern troops marching through its streets in April 1865, and the Civil War ended six days later when Robert E. Lee surrendered to Union General Ulysses Grant at Appomattox, about ninety miles west. The city exuded the eeriness of being painfully trapped beneath the historic weights of slavery and oppression. Ghosts of the past hid everywhere.

To make ends meet, I'd taken a temporary legal job paying twenty-three dollars an hour a few weeks earlier. For eight hours every day, I read hundreds of pages of numbingly tedious legal jargon pertaining to how a certain mechanical device worked. Sitting in my assigned cubicle while a supervisor inspected from the front of the room, my soul slowly died.

Applying for any university job I could find, I desperately

yearned to make the transition from politics to higher education. But I needed money now; otherwise, I would not be able to pay rent. Or eat.

As I picked at my sandwich during my thirty-minute lunch break, I could not hold in the sobs any longer, and when they came, they came. I wailed, rocking back and forth on the bank building's top step. I did not care who saw me. My sandwich became soggy from tears and humidity. When I looked down at my watch, I saw I had four and a half minutes to get back to my cubicle before I would be docked pay. I got up to throw my paper bag in the metal trash can on the sidewalk and wiped my face with a piece of tissue from my pocket. Then I walked through the glass double doors, the air-conditioning hitting me like oncoming traffic.

SCENE THREE: MEMOIR PART I

January 2005 (Age 33)

I finished the first version of my memoir on a January evening. At 10:15 the next morning, I carefully tucked my pages into a large white envelope and hopped into a cab. The driver looked back at me in his rearview mirror. "Where are we headed today?"

I repeated the address I had typed on the envelope's label. It was the law office of the literary agent I most wanted to represent me, and it was only a few blocks from the law firm where I worked in Washington, DC.

The driver sighed at the prospect of a short ride and low fare.

"Yes, I know it's close," I said, "but it's very cold today."

I caught him rolling his eyes, an expression he undoubtedly used often with all the well-heeled lawyers in Washington, DC, such as myself.

When the light turned green, the taxi began moving east. I

rubbed my hands together to warm them. My Burberry wool coat was tied around my waist, and my stiletto boots pinched my feet. An in-person manuscript drop-off to a literary agent was unusual, and even as naive and unseasoned as I was back then, I knew this. Aspiring authors emailed their manuscripts. But I hoped my appearance might work in my favor. Looking the part of a political DC lawyer might inspire the agent to pull my manuscript from the mountain of weekly submissions he undoubtedly received.

As we passed the White House, I looked down at the envelope resting on my lap. How many White House staffers had I written about in these pages? Five? During the campaign, I'd spoken with senior White House staffers many times each day.

A moment later, we arrived at my destination, an office building of towering stone and glass.

"Here you are, young lady."

"Thank you," I said, handing him a ten-dollar bill. "Have a nice day."

I got out and stood on the sidewalk, craning my neck to look at the building. Despite working in DC for years, I had never been here. I drew in a deep breath to steady myself, wondering if finally, *finally*, my new life was about to begin. After starting my book in Australia and spending a year incessantly writing, rewriting, and editing, my memoir was now finished. This crisp white envelope contained 93,500 words. I clasped it with my slightly trembling hands.

I pulled open the heavy double doors and walked into the elevator. As the only person inside, I felt free to check out my appearance in the elevator-door mirrors. I was tall and thin with long, dark-blonde hair and expectant hazel-green eyes, and my outfit looked perfect. I adjusted the belt on my coat and shifted my feet in my boots before the doors reopened. I walked confidently into the lobby, the loud *click-click-click* of my stilettos ringing across the marble floor.

"May I help you?" said the woman sitting at a large desk.

"Yes. I'm here to drop my manuscript off."

I looked down at the white envelope in my hands as she stared at me. *She's sizing me up rather impatiently*, I thought. *She must not realize my book has never been in the hands of a stranger before. Be brave, Jen. You must be brave.*

Deep down, I realized I was the bravest person I knew. These past years had proven as much. I squared my shoulders and, with enormous determination, held out the envelope.

She looked at the agent's name on the label and smiled at me.

"Thank you very much," she said, putting me at ease with her friendly demeanor. "You can leave this with me. I'll make sure he sees it."

"Thank you" was all I said. I mustered a slight smile before turning back toward the elevator and pressing the down button. Once safely inside, I leaned my forehead against the elevator's cold, shiny gold trim, and it steadied me.

A few days later, I was shocked when I got an email from the agent. I had not expected a reply so quickly. He wrote that my book was very good, but he typically represented only very famous clients. His email confused me. Did he want to represent me? How should I reply? As I was mulling this over, I received a very unusual call. The chairman of my law firm asked to meet with me—not in his office or mine but in a tiny conference room I'd never been inside before. When we met, he sat in one chair, and I sat in another, facing him. As soon as we were situated, he turned toward me.

"Jen, have you written a book?"

Icy-cold fright from the surprise paralyzed the muscles in my face, and for a few seconds, I could not speak. I looked at him. As a seasoned lawyer, I knew he was closely observing my response. His stare penetrated mine. Was I being recorded in this odd little room?

"Yes." I thought telling the truth was paramount, although I didn't know why.

"What is it about?" He said this sternly, his steely gray eyes never leaving my face.

"About me and my life."

"We do not take kindly to this," he said.

"I don't understand. Why?" In fact, I did understand, but I wanted to draw him out. "This book is about *me* and *my* experiences."

"Do you mention anyone affiliated with this firm, or people we work with in politics?"

I paused. "Yes," I said.

"Uh-huh," he responded knowingly. We sat in silence for a long time. I willed myself not to fill the silence with words.

At last, he spoke. "You can leave now."

Two weeks later, on the afternoon of February 2, 2005, I resigned. I also learned that the agent was not going to represent me.

Two years later, another firm employee revealed that these two men—the literary agent and the chairman—were friends. Not only that, but the literary agent's secretary—the woman to whom I'd nervously handed my white envelope—had worked as the chairman's secretary years earlier and had called him to spill the beans about my book.

The ordeal terrified me. I had been intimidated by two Washington, DC, power brokers who scared me so much that I did not write one word about the campaign for almost twenty years, and I have never shared that manuscript with anyone since.

For years, I was filled with the kind of nonsensical thoughts that grow in the psyche of a less powerful person (usually a woman) when she is gaslit (usually by a man) and made to believe she is the problem. I grew paranoid, truly believing that the firm or others would come after me, especially when Jim ran for reelection to the Senate in 2006 and lost. I feared for my career, and more than once, I thought I saw people spying on me. I have had countless hours of spiritual and physical therapy along with psychotherapy, but still, to this day, an alarm bell often goes off in my head when my phone rings, telling me that the law firm is calling to destroy me. I know my fears make no sense, and I've learned ways of coping around things that trigger me. I believed I was a worthless, disloyal traitor when, in fact, the opposite has always been true about me, despite my many faults.

SCENE FOUR: RUNNING

December 2002 (Age 31)

I landed in Melbourne, Australia, on an overcast Wednesday during the first week of December in 2002, the beginning of the Australian summer. I took a cab from the airport to the university apartment. I dropped my bags inside, found my running clothes, and went for a seven-mile run through sheets of pouring rain. For the first time in over sixteen months, I began to feel free.

I planned to use the visiting professorship to have time and space to write. I started working on my memoir on a mid-December morning in my University of Melbourne Law School office. Staring out the window onto a sun-drenched sidewalk, I was alone in the deepest sense of that word. Most faculty members and students had left campus for the summer holiday, and it was so quiet it frightened me. Noise had been my constant companion for the fifteen months that I managed the campaign. Now, all day long, I was alone.

Time Bomb: Five. Four. Three. Two. One. Boom.

When the idea came to me about how to start my book, I wrote a sentence, thinking I could always change the words later. It turned out that this was one of only a few lines I have never touched in all my later drafts:

> *At the time, I didn't see it as the moment to remember, my moment, the one that would separate me from my former life forever.*

I had no idea how much truth lived in that one line.

SCENE FIVE: BURNED

April 2002 (Age 30)

For an entire week, I lived on the floor of my St. Louis apartment, fully clothed, totally alone, and in debilitating pain. I had moved to St. Louis from Washington, DC, to live the life I'd dreamed of, sacrificed everything for, and spent a decade working incessantly to achieve. I'd risen to become one of the most successful and powerful women in Republican politics. At the very same time, I felt the weight of the past months. They had been the hardest of my life. My name had been disparagingly plastered on the front pages of newspapers, I'd been sued, my husband and I had divorced, and then there was my car accident—after which, nothing remained the same.

My spine pressed into my apartment's carpeted floor, and my hands fell limp at my sides. I did not change position for several days. Lying on the floor was far more comfortable than sitting or standing. Hour after hour, I gazed upward, seeing objects in my apartment as if for the first time. Everything in my empty bedroom was beige. Beige carpet, beige paint, beige comforter, beige window blinds. My high-heeled gold-and-black snakeskin boots, loosely wrapped in the clear plastic bag from the hospital, looked out of place. They leaned against the beige wall without a cent of value, two burned, mangled remnants of a previous life. Still, I kept them.

From my spot on the ground, I looked up at the orange bottle of prescription painkillers on the counter, but I did not touch them. The voice of religious judgment that had been instilled in me during childhood raged against taking them. The condemnation rang like a bell in my ears.

Because of the pain, I slid through my apartment on my back, propelling myself with my heels. I glided to the refrigerator, and across the room to the sliding glass doors so I could feel the sunshine streaming through the windows, and all the way to the front door to retrieve the food and flowers that had been dropped off by colleagues whose calls I did not return. My colleagues at the White House left three voicemails to ask if I'd received the flowers they sent and inquire about when I would be back at work. I did not listen to the messages for ten days.

I grasped to hang on to my most attractive, reliable qualities—success, virtue, beauty. Now, they felt foreign and hollow. When I stared at my face in the mirror to resurrect myself, I saw only a void. Eyes glared back at me, but they were not my own.

My new reality foretold a radical truth. My soul would not stay quiet and hidden forever, no matter how effectively I'd ignored it. I could not reason away, talk away, or pray away who my soul was or what she was trying to tell me.

In the end, the soul will have her say.

CHAPTER 2

Becoming Wired

THE MONSTER

January 1997 (Age 25)

The happiest day of my life was January 9, 1997, my first day working for Congressman Jim Talent on Capitol Hill. I woke at 5:00 a.m., dressed in my best suit, and rode the Blue Line to the Capitol South Metro station. I exited the underground train and hopped onto the escalator for the steep ride to the surface. As the 350-step escalator inched upward, I clutched tightly to the railing. It was so steep and treacherously high that I felt sure I would fall. Not wanting to appear foolish, I held my terror in check and glanced nervously around me, my eyes screaming at fellow passengers, *Are you seeing how steep this is?!* They were unfazed. When the escalator finally spit me out onto the street-level platform, I cautiously turned to look down. I felt off balance when I couldn't see the bottom. It suddenly occurred to me that thousands of commuters made that same journey every day without a moment's concern. I smoothed the wrinkles in my long coat and straightened my shoulders. *I work in the nation's capital now*, I thought. *Playing it cool on the metro is just a part of what important people do.*

I walked toward South Capitol Street. When I turned the corner, the magnificent dome of the United States Capitol came into full view, soaring overhead. I paused, my breath catching as I stood in awe. The morning sunlight illuminated the dome as streams of beautifully dressed people passed me at an urgent clip.

After dreaming about this day for months, I knew I did not have a moment to waste when it finally came. With fifteen thousand congressional staffers and four thousand interns working in Congress, distinguishing myself was a lofty goal.

From my very first day, no one could have worked harder than I did. Always the first person to arrive at the office and the very last to leave, my work ethic intensified to a frenzy on Capitol Hill. Within two weeks, I'd researched every piece of legislation Jim had introduced. Within three, I'd read all his floor speeches and press releases from the last six years.

In time, my hard work got noticed, and Jim gave me increasingly important and visible tasks. The more I accomplished, the more it drove me. I worked incessantly, often eighty or more hours a week. I worked on Christmas, Thanksgiving, New Year's; it didn't matter. I did not attend social events, drink alcohol, or go to parties with my colleagues. I worked, and I worked hard.

But in moments of quiet, when I was alone, I felt pieces of myself becoming consumed by a gripping fear of failure. My fears grew into a raging monster that roared with an unstoppable push to succeed. My desire to get ahead did not feel like a gentle needling. It felt like a pounding, and it would bang on my insides like a gong. I would hear the gong go off: *BANG! BANG! BANG!* Gripping inner panic would cover me like a sheet of Saran Wrap, suffocating me. The Monster would yell, *You're not moving fast enough. Other people are passing you by. Move, Jen! Move!*

I could feel The Monster consuming me. She was always there, like a current in a river. I kept my outer image intact even as my insides raged. I did not want anyone to know. But inside, I felt like I would die if I did not find a way to be the most celebrated legal staffer. I had to get ahead.

CHAPTER 3

The Monster Unleashed

TALENT

1997–1998 (Age 26)

A rising star in Congress, Jim Talent was an exceptionally brilliant lawyer, and everyone knew it. He was only thirty-six in 1992 when he was sworn in as the United States congressman from Missouri's second district, and he quickly made a name for himself. As a freshman congressman, he authored the massive welfare overhaul legislation that was ultimately signed into law by President Bill Clinton in 1994. Within four years, House Speaker Newt Gingrich appointed him chairman of the House Small Business Committee.

A staunch and proud conservative, Jim also possessed a disarming sense of humor and an uncanny ability to remain calm in the middle of heated arguments without drawing ire from either side. In Jim's suburban swing district outside of St. Louis, he won reelection to Congress four times in a row despite being significantly outspent by opponents with more well-known last names. Voters genuinely liked him, which spoke volumes about Jim as both a man and a politician.

Jim saw something special in me from our very first days together. I was the youngest lawyer on his staff, but he singled me out for the most important opportunities. In the early months, he asked me to try my hand at drafting his speeches. I spent hours writing and refining them before handing them over for his review. He would return them with so much red ink I could barely discern my original words. But I did not stop trying, and he did not give up on me. Within a few months, I improved.

He found new tasks for me, and I worked harder than anyone to master them. Jim was a labor lawyer by training, so labor law became my specialty even though I had not taken even one labor law class during law school. My work ethic and constant drive impressed him. After one year, I unofficially rose to being Jim's right-hand attorney. As lead counsel for the majority of his committee hearings, I sat next to him on the Congressional Hearing Room's raised dais along with the other members of Congress. The sense of importance only added to my obsessive drive.

Our hearings became bastions for the conservative business community that cheered on our pro-management stance. We did serious battle with the liberals in President Clinton's Labor Department on regulations involving workplace safety. Jim and I hauled more Clinton administration Labor secretaries and undersecretaries to testify on Capitol Hill than any other congressional committee. This rubbed many more important congressmen the wrong way as they were getting outflanked by our aggressive tactics. We were also making headlines. After several months, our Committee Hearing Room audience became standing room only.

My star rose alongside Jim's. Conservative business groups invited me to speak at their conferences around the United States, and the Senate's Republican leadership task force included me as a standing member on labor issues. I was getting noticed.

DRIVE

December 2000 (Age 29)

I left Congress in 2000, the same year Jim ran for Missouri governor. A DC law firm had been pursuing me for several months. McDermott Will & Emery was the world's third-largest law firm, and they offered to double my congressional salary if I joined them.

In the back of my mind, I wondered why they were so interested in me. I was good at my job—sure. But there were dozens of outstanding lawyers on Capitol Hill. Three months in, I got my answer when the managing partner asked me to come to his office.

"There's been an explosion at a chemical plant in Texas," he told me. "One man has been killed, and many others received severe burns. A complicating factor is that the deceased employee was injured in 1989 in a similar explosion at the same plant."

He looked at me. I did not know what to say, so I nodded to show I was listening.

"I'll be traveling to Houston for three days every week for the next year to represent the chemical company, and I want you to come with me."

I took a deep breath and felt a wave of revulsion. The managing partner was staring at me. To fill the silence, I said, "Thank you for the opportunity." Then I looked down at my Gucci shoes.

For the next eight months, a black Lincoln Town Car picked me up at my house to take me to the airport at 5:00 a.m. every Tuesday morning. I flew on the same United flight to Houston in the same first-class seat—1B—where I was greeted by the same flight attendants who always gave me a ceramic mug of coffee and a croissant. The Four Seasons hotel staff in downtown Houston knew me by name.

There were no shades of gray about expectations. The chemical company paid me hundreds of dollars an hour to represent them with the same pro-management aggressiveness I'd demonstrated in Congress. For the first few months, I really tried. Reviewing hundreds of boxes of documents and interviewing employee witnesses, I worked diligently to string together strong legal arguments. But I couldn't do it. My work would ultimately be used against the dead and suffering employees, which made me feel like I had caused the explosion, or worse, that I was detonating it all over again. It was one thing to be celebrated in the media for skewering a government official before Congress, but it was quite another to walk through buildings where people had died in an explosion and others remained hospitalized with agonizing burns. I felt the crippling glances of fury, fear, and sadness from the employees who remained. Their stares penetrated me even if I pretended otherwise. At the same time, I developed a debilitating fear of flying. I cried in my hotel room every night. In the mornings, I had to force myself to leave the hotel to go to the plant. Deep down, I knew I was a fake.

In January 2001, after Jim had been narrowly defeated in his race for Missouri governor, he called me. Another DC law firm wanted to hire him, and he asked if I would consider jumping firms to join him there. I did not hesitate for even one second.

"Yes," I said. "When do we start?"

AMBITION

May–July 2001 (Age 29)

Jim Talent's Senate campaign began with a phone call.

In May 2001, President George W. Bush called Jim one afternoon to encourage him to run for Senate. Their private conversation lasted about fifteen minutes, and after it was done, he came into my office.

"So, what did President Bush say, Jim?"

"He told me that his White House team crunched the polling numbers, and I am the only Republican who can win the Missouri Senate race next year."

"That's incredible. What did you say?"

"I told him I'd think about it."

"That's it? That's all you said?"

"Yes. What else could I have said? I'm not going to pull one over on the president of the United States."

After winning so many congressional elections in a row, Jim's confidence had been bruised when he lost the 2000 gubernatorial race. No one could have foreseen what happened in Missouri that year. Three weeks before Election Day, the sitting governor of Missouri—Democrat Mel Carnahan—died in a plane crash. He was running for Senate and was flying across the state as part of his campaign to beat the incumbent senator, John Ashcroft. Carnahan's son had been the plane's pilot, and he died, too. Waves of sympathy flooded in to support Mel's widow, Jean Carnahan. That same sympathy also boosted Democrats running for election across Missouri—including the Democrat running against Jim. After a series of complicated political events, Jim lost the governor's race, and Mel Carnahan beat Senator John Ashcroft posthumously. The new governor (who had served as lieutenant governor under Mel Carnahan) appointed Mrs. Carnahan to serve two years in the United States Senate in lieu of her husband. Because she was appointed, and not elected, Mrs. Carnahan would have to run again in 2002 to fill the rest of the Senate term. Jean Carnahan was the Democrat that President Bush wanted Jim to beat.

On the day President Bush called, Jim was forty-five years old and had served in elected federal and state political roles for sixteen years. The possibility of running for the Senate—and losing—petrified him. Popular politicians are allowed one loss in their careers; after two, they are considered has-beens.

For the next three months, Jim and I had variations of the same conversation again and again. They went like this:

"I am not sure how I'm supposed to run against a widow who deserves our sympathy. Voters still feel grief for her, and rightly so. Not only that, but she's a grandmother. How is it going to look for me to beat up on a widow and a grandmother?!"

"You are not going to beat up on her, Jim. You're going to highlight that she was *appointed* to the Senate by a Democratic governor when her husband died. She has never been elected to anything. She has zero governing experience. We can be respectful toward her while reminding the voters of the facts."

"Still, she's now *Senator* Carnahan."

"Sure, but she's only had that title for *one* year. That is an honor she was given and did not earn."

"I don't think I can win against a woman who is so beloved in Missouri."

"Of course you can, and it's not just me saying it. President Bush himself has said this to you. He and his team think you can win."

"It's no skin off his nose if I lose, Jen. This is my career. My life!"

Patience was my tactic. The saying goes that every House member wants to become a senator, and every senator wants to be president, and Jim was no exception. But I knew he had to find his way there by himself. The clock, however, was ticking. If Jim decided to enter the race, he'd need to make up his mind by the end of July to start raising money as a Senate candidate who was financially competitive against Jean Carnahan—who surely would raise tens of millions of dollars. Until then, I let him exorcise his fears on me as often as he needed to.

On the last Tuesday in July, I was in my office when my cell phone rang. I looked at the caller ID and closed my eyes. Today was the day.

I picked up the phone.

"Jim?"

"Jen, I've made my decision." He paused for a long time, and through the phone, I could hear him tapping his fingers. To steady myself, I focused my attention on a spot on the wall across the room.

"I've decided to do it. I'm going to run for the Senate."

I put my face in my hands before lowering my head to the lip of my desk, the cool wood pressing against my forehead. I had not realized I'd stopped breathing until the air poured from my mouth all at once, making a sound like wind in a tunnel. I let my head rest there as Jim continued talking.

"But here's the thing. I can't do it without you. I need you here in St. Louis to assemble the team and manage them . . . and, I guess, to manage me, too. Will you come?"

I let the joy of hearing these words flow through me for a few seconds before I threw my right hand above my body, punching the air in victory with such force that I almost toppled backward out of my desk chair.

"Yes, Jim. Yes, I'll come. You know I'll come."

"Thank you, Jen. That is outstanding. Wonderful!" Jim paused for a moment. "When will you tell John?"

I took a deep breath and closed my eyes. John was my husband at the time.

"Soon, Jim. I'll handle it." I did not sound even marginally convincing, but Jim had already moved on.

"Here we go, Jen."

"Wow, Jim. Here we go."

When I hung up, I stood, threw my arms in the air, and

danced around my office, mimicking Rocky Balboa at the top of the Philadelphia Museum of Art steps. I wanted to scream with delight and run down the law firm halls sharing the news, but, of course, I couldn't tell anyone. It was late July, and we would not release the announcement for at least a week.

Managing a Senate campaign of this caliber was a dream come true for me, and it carried the promise of fulfilling another dream: to be a chief of staff in the US Senate.

SEX

June 2001 (Age 29)

John and I lived in Deale, a tiny fishing village on the Chesapeake Bay, about thirty miles southeast of Washington, DC. The commuter traffic could be horrendous, especially at rush hour. But that was never a problem for me, given that I never traveled at rush hour; I always left the house at sunrise and returned home long after dinnertime.

When I walked in, I heard John's squeaky desk chair move in his home office.

"Jen, is that you?"

"Who else would it be?" I laughed. "Have a minute?"

Two months earlier, we had traveled to Italy for two weeks in an attempt to rekindle feelings between us. It was the place I'd longed to go more than anywhere else in the world, and I'd prayed I would find it romantic. Starting in Rome, we made our way south through Naples to the Amalfi Coast. For five days, we stayed at Le Sirenuse, a five-star hotel hanging from the cliffs over the Tyrrhenian Sea. Our sunny Positano balcony was dotted with lemon trees and pink bougainvillea spilling over the railings.

There could not be a more romantic place in the world, I tried to convince myself. But the thing I remember most from that trip is opening our room's balcony door each night to hear the echoing sound of waves reverberating through the half dome of the cliffs. John would be sound asleep, exhausted from arguing about the sex we never had, and I looked out at the sea and wondered what was wrong with me.

We had not had sex in five years. John and I lived as married friends, and because I was loyal to my vows, I stayed with him.

Now, two months later, I was about to tell him I was leaving him. I was twenty-nine years old and desperate to get away. Pursuing my dream job was the perfect opportunity, an acceptable excuse to leave without leaving my marriage. After all, I would only be gone for fifteen months. In the dream I'd concocted, I would return to DC as the chief of staff to a United States senator, and that would require me to work harder than ever.

I told him about Jim's decision to run for the Senate.

"He's asked me to move to Missouri," I said, looking straight at him.

My nature is to tackle difficult subjects head-on, but I struggled to describe why I, of all people, needed to move to Missouri. With zero campaign expertise and, at best, only a cursory knowledge of Missouri geography and politics, Jim did not need me to win the race. Where I added value was knowing Jim the Politician—how he thought about issues, his strategic sensibilities, his vision for the future. I explained, but I could tell John did not buy it.

He responded with only three words: "For how long?"

"Only fifteen months," I said. "I'll leave at the end of August and be back after the election next November."

John's eyes lit up with anger, which surprised me. He slowly set his white coffee mug on his desk before standing up. His eyes shot rage in my direction. As he passed me in the doorway on his way out of the office, he glared into my face, his temper simmering just below the surface. He was ready to explode.

"You're such a bitch." He seethed as he grabbed the keys to his truck and walked out of the house.

I did not see him again for two weeks.

MAKING PLANS

August 1983 (Age 11)

To understand how I grew up to live a life that was not entirely my own, one must look at all the times I learned to betray myself, starting at a very young age.

In my family, a clear line existed between the things that mattered and those that did not. Priorities were not written down; they didn't need to be. My father drilled them into me with military precision. Acceptable pathways to winning his approval included hard work and success. Pursuing other paths led to being chastised or ignored.

I lived on both sides of the line. As a child, I was a disappointment. A tomboy who cared most about building forts, climbing trees, and singing along to recordings of Broadway musicals, I wrote adventure stories and specialized in playing pretend. I was an average student at best. Every red C scribbled atop the tests I brought home caused my father's heart to sink further.

I was eleven years old the first time my father brought me into his office to have The Talk. No one entered this forbidden territory unless invited, and I walked in with trepidation. My family had recently moved to Traverse City, Michigan, and I would start sixth grade at my new school in a few weeks.

"Have a seat." My father pointed to the wooden chair across from him.

I must be in trouble, I thought. I was never there for any other reason. We stared at one another for a few moments before my father cleared his throat.

"Jen," he started. "Why are you doing what you're doing?"

Before being called into his office, I had been playing pretend with plastic toys on my bedroom desk and writing about it. I wondered why my father was asking me about this. Because I didn't know what else to say, I decided to tell him the truth.

"I was making a scene from the Wild West and writing a story about a cowgirl who decided to become a pirate."

A confused expression landed on my father's face. "No, no. What I mean is, what do you want to do with the rest of your life?"

I knew it was ridiculous to ask someone my age this question. But my father was serious, and his gaze left no room for anything but a stellar answer. Like him, I also hoped that I could procure something meaningful from the recesses of my brain. The sum of my goals was making friends at my new school, but that did not seem like the kind of response my dad was looking for.

His dark brown eyes bored into my face as if they were drill bits. I'd feared my father for as long as I could remember, but I'd taught myself to conjure up my instinct for bravery whenever I was before him. I took a deep breath and slowly released the air to steady myself.

"I want to be a singer," I blurted. This response surprised my dad. "I want to be a lawyer" or "I hope to be a nuclear physicist" would have impressed him; singing did not. I knew he'd heard me singing along to my *West Side Story* record for hours every day, but my talents must not have been persuasive. He swiveled away from me in his chair so I could no longer see his face.

My father's intensity was legendary. As a young man, in the span of only four years, he went from trying out to be a pitcher for the Chicago Cubs to piloting bomber jets through the mountains at night during the Vietnam War. He graduated from Northwestern University's Kellogg School of Management and worked as a senior marketing executive. Succeeding in all areas of life was fundamentally important to him, particularly as it related to his children.

"What are your next steps?" He turned toward me and removed a tablet of goldenrod legal paper from his desk drawer. At the top, he wrote *GOALS* in capital letters. He underlined the word twice. It took fifteen minutes for us to map out the next twenty years of my life. We filled the paper with my step-by-step tactics. Singing lessons. Guitar lessons. Auditioning for plays. Researching the best music schools. I didn't know much about how to achieve the goals we wrote down, but I went along for the ride, hoping it would secure the soonest possible release from his office.

He tore the sheet from his legal pad and handed it to me. "Keep this somewhere you'll see it every day to remember your goals."

Back in my bedroom, I folded the paper in half and tucked it into my desk drawer in case my dad ever asked to see it again. As I sat in my chair replaying our conversation, I noticed a stirring inside of me. There was pressure in the hollow of my chest, and the pace of my breathing accelerated. I put my hand on the corner of my desk, my fingers shaking slightly. Inside my mind, someone began speaking, and the tone of her voice frightened me. *You are a failure*, she hissed. *You'd better get moving.* I didn't know it then, but the voice belonged to The Monster.

Over time, I replaced my dirty Wranglers and flannel shirts with skinny jeans and designer blazers. My boyishly tall frame became noticeably statuesque, and the blonde highlights I added to my hair accentuated my olive skin. Because most uncomfortable truths can be hidden behind facades of beauty, this was how I hid The Monster.

REWARDS

1978 (Age 7)

Even as a young girl, I knew The Monster's existence was tied to having an obsessively driven and successful father. His demands, combined with growing up surrounded by the trappings of achievement, set a high bar for expectations. I also witnessed how The Monster exacted its price.

I understood that all the houses my family lived in when I was growing up and the furnishings inside them were the hallmarks of rich people. My dad worked for the World Dryer corporation, and my family lived in a beautiful brick home on Maple Street in Hinsdale, Chicago's wealthiest suburb. I clearly recall the day when contractors showed up at our front door to install World Dryers in each of our bathrooms, just like the wall mounted, hand-push dryers in restaurants. I instantly became a standout celebrity in the first grade. In a town so affluent that new sports cars barely turned heads, my friends fought over who would get to come home with me after school to play with the dryers. I coined my home the World Dryer House, and just like Buckingham Palace or Graceland, the name stuck.

Our monthly electric bills must have been staggering that year because I ran the World Dryer in my bathroom nonstop. Barbies were melted under its piercing heat, and I used the unit to dry my entire body after taking a bath, pressing the button over and over again until my skin was as hot as a Thanksgiving turkey. I styled my hair by flipping the nozzle upward to concentrate the blowing heat, making myself resemble Billy Idol long before I knew who he was.

A year later, we moved. For my dad, the next rung up the corporate ladder was serving as senior vice president at a large Michigan-based toy company. My younger brother and I could not believe our eyes when we came home from school one day to see a fully assembled Lionel Train setup in our basement. It was the size of a small swimming pool and included model towns and mountains, lakes and rivers, conductors who waved when the trains went by, and places on the track that made steam puff from the train's engine.

"Don't ever forget how hard your dad works for our family," our mom said to us while we fiddled with the remote controls to race the trains. "This train set proves how much he loves you."

THE VOICE OF GOD

1983 (Age 11)

When my faith in God wavered, which it sometimes did, one memory from my childhood always gave me strength.

Inside a beautiful log cabin–style building on a campus at the edge of Lake Michigan, six small children, my brother, and I were playing in what was known as the piano room. I was eleven, my brother was nine, and the children in my babysitting charge ranged in age from three to eight years old. We'd moved to Northern Michigan a year or so earlier, when my dad changed jobs again—he now served as the president of a boarding high school. He was leading a meeting in the school's student center, and these children's parents—administrators and teachers—were in attendance. I babysat while they met in an adjacent room.

The kids and I sat on a circular carpet that covered the tile floor. Two played with Legos, and one colored quietly with a stack of crayons pulled from a small green bucket. The girls next to me played cat's cradle with a piece of string. Half of my attention was on teaching them to delicately grab and pull the string through their fingers, and the other half was on a three-year-old boy who was running around the room at top speed, yelling

"Ahhhhhhh!" at the top of his lungs. His constant screaming was annoying everyone, and besides, I didn't want the parents to think I couldn't handle a three-year-old child.

I stood up, and the boy sped up when he saw me, racing even faster toward the piano. I ran after him, catching him by the shoulders. That's when he turned toward me. I saw he was holding a long plastic coffee stirrer just before he jammed it into my eye. I screamed and fell backward into the wall. I thought my eye might fall out of its socket, but as I pressed my fingertips against my lid, it seemed like it was still in place. It throbbed with tremendous pain. My brother ran into the next room to get my dad, who came into the piano room to get me.

During our thirty-minute drive home, my dad instructed me to pray. As much as my eye hurt, there was never any thought—his or mine—of going to a hospital. We believed fully in the power of prayer to heal. Mark and I sat in the back seat of my dad's car. With my eyes closed, I felt the gentle pitch and sway of the car on the country roads. I tried to settle my mind and ignore the pain, but I was afraid. No one spoke. I heard the whir of the engine and the tires on the pavement. But gradually, I became aware of a voice inside the car singing a hymn from Sunday school, and I thought it was my dad. I listened, and when he finished, I leaned into the front seat.

"Thank you for singing, Dad."

He turned his head just enough for me to see his eyes squinch in disbelief. "You heard singing?" He was incredulous. Clearly, he had not been singing, and his response unsettled me. I leaned back into my seat at the same moment my brother piped up.

"I heard it, too!" Mark chimed in. "The person singing 'O Gentle Presence'!"

I had not said the name of the hymn I'd heard to either Mark or my dad, and Mark's confirmation that he'd heard it, too, felt like magic falling from the sky. I was sure we'd just been visited by the divine. Someone, and I believed it was God, had sung that hymn for my brother and me to hear. When we arrived home and I looked in the bathroom mirror, my eye had only the tiniest speck of red remaining in the corner. The pain was gone.

Ever since, this experience has stood as a beacon of faith for me. In times of doubt and fear, I remember that my hard work and devotion resulted in God singing to me and healing my eye. This is my model for how Christian Science—and life—is supposed to work.

SEEDS

1978–1989 (Ages 7–18)

Being a Christian Scientist meant I attracted unwanted attention. When people learned about my religion, I became known as "that girl who doesn't go to doctors." I hated standing out in this way.

When I was a teenager, I did my best to hide my religion. I successfully managed this because our family moved so often due to my dad's changing jobs. Before I graduated from high school, I'd attended nine schools in seven cities and four states. This dizzying experience forced me to learn the best way to hot-wire myself into new friendship circuits like a master, becoming the most popular girl in school by quickly acquiring the local accent along with my new friends' music and clothing tastes. I became a shape-shifter, and in the process, I often felt very lost and confused about who I was. Even so, I never completely abandoned myself. In the rare moments when I remembered to turn inward, I burned with a sense of my own knowing that felt fierce and ferocious. I was just too scared to trust it most of the time.

Starting in second grade, no matter where my family lived, I spent almost two months every summer for eight years at Christian Science camp in Northern Michigan. I can still smell the scent of the pine trees and hear the waves lapping up on the Lake Michigan shoreline. Every morning, the campers and I walked single file down the dirt path leading from our cabins to the lake as sunlight poked through the trees. The birds tweeted above us in the tall birches, maples, and red pines, and when I looked up, I sometimes saw one fly between the swaying branches. I felt like I was part of the forest, of God, too, and that God was a part of me. At camp, quiet was part of the natural rhythm of things. Time was everywhere as much as it was nowhere, and beauty surrounded us. God never talked to me about not going to doctors or following rules when I was at camp. What came alive was the importance of following my own inner light. At the time, I equated my camp experiences of God with my devotion to Christian Science. But in time, I came to see that these summers were the beginning of my spiritual becoming on my own terms.

As a child, I could not detect the difference between what I knew deep down to be true, my *own* knowing, and the religious rules about medicine and healing. I had been carefully and lovingly taught that they were one and the same. Our example was set by a Bible story found in the book of Matthew. A father asked Jesus's disciples to heal his son's mental illness. The disciples prayed and prayed, but they could not heal the boy. When an exasperated Jesus entered the scene, he immediately healed the child.

"Why weren't we successful?" the downtrodden disciples asked Jesus.

"Because you have so little faith," Jesus replied. "Truly, I tell you, if you have faith as small as a mustard seed, you can say to this mountain, 'Move from here to there,' and it will move. Nothing will be impossible for you."

I didn't know what was wrong with the disciples, but I was sure my own faith could easily fill a minuscule seed. I trusted my faith completely.

When I was a child, the key takeaway of this Bible story was about spirituality. Now that I am an adult, I see the divine fullness of my time at camp and how it shaped me. Hiking through dense forests with only the sound of the birds singing, sailing across the whitecaps of Grand Traverse Bay, building campsites on sandy beaches using twigs and twine, picking so many Michigan cherries from the surrounding trees that my fingers and lips turned purple, God was always with me, quietly telling me about myself. Paula D'Arcy writes that God comes to us disguised as our own lives, and I now know I developed my sense of who I was during those summers. My independence, my fierceness, and the spark of fire and energy that is my personality were all formed at camp, tied to a poetic love of landscape that grounds me to this day. It would take me many years to understand this, but looking back now, I am so overwhelmed by the beauty of this truth that it makes me weep.

THORNS

August 2001 (Age 29)

I boarded a plane for St. Louis in early August, seven days after informing John of my plans to run Jim's Senate campaign. I still hadn't laid eyes on him. I would be there for five days before returning to DC and permanently moving to St. Louis at the end of the month.

I clutched the straps of my carry-on luggage as I inched down the congested airplane aisle. I passed seat 1B, the seat

I'd always occupied on my weekly flights to Houston, and my mind flooded with memories of the fear of flying I'd developed a year ago. It made me laugh, certain I must be the plane's only coach passenger who was happy not to be sitting in first class. After I left McDermott, my fear of flying immediately vanished, and I regained my love of traveling.

When I got to Row 14, I shoved my luggage inside the overhead compartment and sat down in my window seat to check my BlackBerry. The first email I saw was from Jim:

Jen,

Brenda and I are wondering if you are in St. Louis yet. Call me when you arrive.

Jim

I typed back:

Hi Jim,

I'm on the plane, about to take off. I'll be arriving in STL this afternoon. I'll call you.

Jen

I was the fastest Blackberry typist I knew, but my left thumb struggled to hit the letters on the keypad. Every time I extended my thumb, I felt a painful throbbing. I inspected my fingers in the sunlight of the airplane window and saw a small red bump just below the nail. I touched it and flinched. Then, I remembered what had happened. Leaving my house that morning, I'd stopped on our front walkway underneath the wrought iron arch covered in pink climbing roses. Walking through the trellis, I'd spotted a dead rose and instinctively grabbed the stem with my bare hands to deadhead the bloom. A thorn had pricked my thumb.

Ah, I thought. *The thorn.* Identifying the cause of my thumb's irritation allowed me to brush the pain aside and forget about it.

But by evening, I could not move my thumb without significant pain. I joined Jim and Brenda for dinner but begged off early. I slowly walked down the stairs to my basement guest room at the friend's house where I was staying, my eyes fixed on my mangled thumb. Standing in the bathroom, I found some gauze and wrapped it tightly. I drifted in and out of sleep that night as the pain pulsed in waves. By morning, oozing pus had turned the cotton a shade of pale yellow. I got out of bed and carefully unwrapped it. My thumb had swollen to three times its normal size.

I gasped. In utter panic, I sat down to pray. I waited for the healing to come. But healing did not come.

Twelve hours later, I succumbed to begging God to stop the pain. The only voice I heard in reply was one of judgment, a voice that sounded a lot like The Monster, or perhaps my own father. Any God who might be with me did not feel like either love or light, and certainly not like the God who had been with me at summer camp.

The next morning, I passed out during my first work meeting.

It was one of the lowest points in my life. Humiliated, abandoned by God, and too embarrassed to ask for help, I drove to the nearest hospital. I kept thinking about the time I'd been poked in the eye with the coffee stirrer and heard the Voice of God.

I remember arriving at the hospital, but nothing after that until I woke up lying on a gurney with a doctor in a white coat standing over me, saying something that I couldn't hear.

"Sorry?" I asked.

He repeated his question. "Why did it take you so long to come to the hospital?"

I was disoriented and confused. I thought he was asking about my work situation. I told him I lived in DC but worked for Jim Talent, and that was why I was in St. Louis.

"Wait." The doctor stopped short. He put his hand on his chest, smoothing his already-crisp white medical coat. "You work for Jim Talent?"

I nodded. He then walked away, taking his phone out of his pocket and closing the curtain behind him. It made the sound of metal on metal, like pulling a shower curtain closed. I looked around at the white walls. A box of purple latex gloves sat on a counter, and a monitor beeped beside me.

A few moments later, the doctor was back in my makeshift room.

"Jim said I am to take very good care of you. I'm going to operate on you right now."

"Jim . . . Jim Talent? You spoke with Jim?"

"Yes. He's one of my closest friends."

Nothing I have ever experienced was more painful than my two-hour thumb operation. I was told later that the infection had seeped into my muscles and bloodstream. Staph infection had set in. This would be the first of two surgeries that Dr. Coin performed on my thumb; the second, at the end of August, repaired the nerve damage and my thumb's appearance. In the interim weeks, I had strict instructions to take antibiotics.

Dr. Coin himself handed me the orange prescription bottles. "Jim told me you aren't someone who normally takes medicine. Is that true?" he asked.

I nodded, utterly defeated. I had never before felt like such a failure. In the course of seven hours, I had lost my lifelong identity as a faithful Christian Scientist because I chose medical attention instead of relying on God for healing. For days, I couldn't shake a certain thought: *What if I didn't get it wrong, but my understanding of God is wrong?* My thoughts about myself, God, and the rules I needed to follow made me feel like my life was ripping apart. I had no idea who I was anymore. All I wanted was to stitch myself back together again.

PROVING MYSELF

September 2001 (Age 30)

Missouri is a land of rivers. In the years before modern transportation came to the Midwest, Missouri's big rivers were its highways, pumping life and commerce into historic towns like Boonville, Cape Girardeau, Hannibal, St. Charles, and St. Louis. To the east, the Mississippi River separates Missouri from Illinois, Kentucky, and Tennessee as it flows southward. Then there's the Mighty Mo, a nickname for the Missouri River, the longest river on the continent. Starting in Montana's Rocky Mountains, it pushes its way south through five states before joining the Mississippi in St. Louis. Together, they form the world's fourth-largest river system. Dozens of other rivers slice through Missouri, too, from the Osage in Lake of the Ozarks to the Black River in Southeast Missouri and the Meramec in the middle of the state. A source of both lore and pride, Missouri's rivers give the state much of its character. The five miles of caves under the Meramec River are said to have been a hideout for the outlaw Jesse James, explorers Lewis and Clark used the Missouri River as a guide for exploring westward, and Mark Twain's novels made the Mississippi legendary.

The four-by-four-foot wall map I'd purchased from Rand McNally helped me learn the names and routes of every river in Missouri. I memorized the names and geographic locations of big and small cities, state parks and natural geologic formations, highways and main thoroughfares cutting through the state, types of Missouri agriculture and crops, and locations of Missouri's biggest churches, farms, Rotary clubs, and farm organizations. Political nerd that I was, I created my own puzzle from cutouts of all of Missouri's 114 counties and did it over and over until I could assemble it perfectly, placing each county in the right place.

In September, I met Lloyd. A sixty-something native Missourian from the farmlands around Cape Girardeau, Lloyd had agreed to help manage Jim's campaign from his home base in Southeast Missouri. Lloyd's legendary status was notable for a few reasons. He knew Missouri politics better than anybody, and it was no secret that he did not like people from Washington, DC.

When I parked my Saab convertible outside the Denny's in St. Charles, I grabbed my umbrella to protect my pinstriped black suit and high-heeled snakeskin boots from the rain. Lloyd and I had talked on the phone at least fifteen times before this morning, and our conversations had always been easy. Not today.

"So, tell me," Lloyd said, staring at me after I sat down in the booth. "What in the hell is a city girl like you doing running a campaign here in Missouri?"

Unrattled, I didn't miss a beat. "I care about Jim and this election. I want him to win."

Lloyd returned to picking at his eggs. He lifted a fork to his face as he leaned toward me, the tines staring at me. "I like Jim," Lloyd said carefully, eggs dripping onto his plate. "What I'm asking is what *you* know about it. You plan to go traipsing through our fields of soybeans and corn in those high-heeled boots, do you?"

I sat up straighter in my seat. I paused, but only for effect. "Lloyd, I can do this."

He looked down at his plate and nodded. My gamble of going toe-to-toe with him had paid off.

"Jen?" Lloyd said, turning to look out the window, staring in the direction of my car.

"Yes?"

"Just lose the freakin' Saab. You're in God's country now. We don't like Swedish cars with windshield wipers on the goddamned headlights."

ALL HAT AND NO CATTLE

September–October 2001 (Age 30)

It was three weeks before Lloyd began to trust me. I knew he'd come around when he left me a voicemail in the middle of October inviting me to dinner. I called him back when I got out of my meeting.

"Hi, Lloyd. I'd love to have dinner with you. What time?"

"Six o'clock."

"Sounds good. Where do you want to go?" I asked.

"I shudder to think that a city girl like you is asking *me* where to have dinner. Careful, or I might choose the Piggly Wiggly."

When Lloyd ordered a twenty-dollar glass of chardonnay at Cardwell's in Frontenac, I was more surprised than if a pig wearing lipstick had run across the restaurant floor. I stole glances at him drinking wine out of the dainty, long-stemmed glass, thinking that no true country bumpkin would know the difference between a Côte Bonneville and a Cakebread chardonnay. He pestered me for an hour to join him in having a glass, and to my own surprise, I ended up ordering one. I could count on one hand the number of times I'd drunk wine at a restaurant and didn't know what to order from the daunting wine list. When the waiter came back to our table, I made it easy on myself.

"I'll have what he's having," I said.

Lloyd looked at me and smiled. "About goddamned time," he said.

Midway through my first and his second glass of wine, Lloyd's expression shifted.

"Jen, I need to talk with you about something."

"Okay, shoot." I leaned toward him.

"I've sliced and diced the numbers every way I can, but I cannot figure out a way for Jim to win this race."

"Lloyd!" His horrifying conclusion shocked me so much that I inadvertently blurted out his name as if he had said something blasphemous.

He tapped his fingers on the table, pausing before speaking again.

"Jean Carnahan is going to raise more money than us—probably a lot more money—and we won't be able to buy as many TV ads as she will. We can't keep up. However . . ." Lloyd paused. "There is one way we might win."

He spoke very slowly, injecting long periods of silence between his statements, like he was dropping bombs and watching them explode.

"Well . . . good God, Lloyd. Spit it out!"

"Okay. Here it is. I need you to get us every important person in Republican politics, bring them to Missouri, and create the largest, splashiest events so that the media will have no choice but to cover them in the newspapers and on TV. This is the only way we can catch up to Jean Carnahan and be on TV as much as she is. We just won't be payin' for it. You get my drift?"

I paused. "Me? You need *me* to do this?"

"Yes. And Jen, I also need you to get us President George W. Bush at least three times before Election Day, once in St. Louis, once in Kansas City, and once in Springfield. Three times. Otherwise, Jim will not win."

One month after 9/11, President Bush's national approval rating was above 90 percent, and in Missouri, it was even higher.

"Oh-kay," I replied slowly, emphasizing each syllable. "That makes sense, I guess. But how will I do that?"

He took another swig of wine and wiped his lips with the back of his hand. "I have no clue," he said casually. "That's your territory. You're the one from DC."

My stomach tightened, and I grabbed the bottom of my chair with both hands to hold myself steady.

"Lloyd, I will do anything you ask. But how am I supposed to do this?"

"Those White House people will like you, Jen. You know shit from Shinola, and that's saying something comin' from me about a DC lawyer. You're smart and pretty, even though I'm not supposed to say things like that. You catch my drift? You are from *their world*. They will listen to you when you ask them. They won't listen to a crotchety old farmer from Sikeston, Missouri, with a size 40 waist who wears dungarees and work boots."

In disbelief, I stared directly at him. What did he want me to do, call the White House switchboard and ask to be connected to Air Force One?

I thought about the task in front of me as Lloyd kept talking. His mood had lightened since passing this buck to me. But I was barely listening as he rambled on, terrified of failing at this monumental task.

"I bet you like those shiny things that dangle from the shirts those hoity-toity White House men wear. What are they called again?" With great dramatic flair, Lloyd pointed to his wrists.

"Cufflinks, Lloyd. They're called cufflinks."

"Yeah, cufflinks. I mean, why the hell don't they just wear buttons? I think the whole lot of them are all hat and no cattle."

He stopped talking. He could tell I was nervous, so he paused and locked eyes with me.

"Jen." He said my name as if his life depended on it. "I need you to do this."

I tasted the bile rising in my throat. Lloyd kept talking. I swallowed a big sip of wine to get the acid taste out of my mouth, but it didn't help.

"You will figure this out. I know you will. Mark my words. You're going to win this race for us."

I was frozen with fear and prayed that he was right.

"I'll do my best, Lloyd."

"Miss Jen," he said. "You're going to knock it out of the park."

SUNFISH

September 1985 (Age 14)

I learned to sail at camp on a little white Sunfish. The boat was so tiny that only the sailing instructor and I could fit inside. On a sunny, nearly windless midsummer day, we sailed out into the Grand Traverse Bay on Lake Michigan. I watched her as she slowly guided the tiller and pulled in the main sheet to capture the wind. When a gust came, she pulled harder, and the boat's port side lifted high into the air. I dragged my fingertips along the water, watching the wake they created. Over many summers, I learned to sail on my own. I loved flying across the open water with the wind in my hair and the rush of the water splashing my face.

When I was fourteen, my mom and I visited one of her friends who lived on Glen Lake, a picturesque lake with views of the Sleeping Bear Sand Dunes in Northern Michigan. Her friend had a Sunfish on her property, and she asked if I would like to take it out for a sail.

"Very much," I said. "Thank you."

The day was warm but overcast as I hauled the boat into the water. The wind pushed at the sail, and I had to quickly jump into the boat while I still had my footing on the sandy lake bottom. Once I was inside, my left hand on the tiller and my right wrapped tightly on the main sheet, the Sunfish took off.

Thirty minutes in, it started to rain. Cold droplets pinged loudly on the fiberglass hull. I had not brought a sweatshirt with me and was starting to get cold, so I changed tack, deciding to turn back. That is when the wind picked up.

Northern Michigan is known for its quickly changing weather and storms that come out of nowhere. As I tried to steer the tiller toward the house, it started raining so hard I lost my bearings. I didn't know where I was. The wind pushed on the fabric of the triangle sail with such force that I almost couldn't hold on. The boat rocked, heeling starboard and then heeling port, and I suddenly forgot how to sail. I was terrified.

I started to pray, but I was so scared I couldn't remember any prayers.

"God, help me!" I cried.

That's when I remembered the Bible story about Jesus and the disciples on a small boat in the Sea of Galilee. When the squall appeared, Jesus calmed the storm. He simply got up, rebuked the wind, and said to the waves, "Quiet! Be still!" Then the wind died down and the sea was completely calm.

My next thought was that Jesus had been sleeping just before he did this. *Sleeping?* I said to myself, my hand still pulling in the line so the boat didn't tip. My hand was now red and raw from holding it so tightly. I couldn't imagine sleeping during a storm like this. I thought I was going to capsize and drown. As

I contemplated this, my boat flew over waves in the usually still waters of Glen Lake.

You don't need to sleep was the idea that came. *You just need to be calm.*

I took a deep breath. My hair was plastered to my face, and I was so wet that I looked like I'd been swimming. I looked up and I briefly closed my eyes. I breathed in again before opening them.

I thought, *Okay. Just sail in one direction. This lake is not big. I'll hit shore soon, and I can figure it out.* I pulled the tiller toward myself to tack, and the boat turned. I looked up again, and right in front of me was my mom's friend's house.

TAKING RISKS

October 2001 (Age 30)

On Capitol Hill, my stellar work had enhanced my reputation and my image as a refined and sophisticated lawyer. My work on the campaign, however, was exactly the opposite. I needed to complete my tasks by any means necessary. Gone were any notions of gracefully learning on the job, earning respect as I went along, and ruffling feathers only when necessary. I operated now as if I had been dropped into a rainforest with camouflage war paint and a machete. I had no compass or understanding of the local language, and I wasn't sure I would survive, but I knew I would die trying.

Knowing what I had to do, I placed more than two dozen phone calls to everyone I knew in DC who might be able to help get President George W. Bush and other senior Republicans to come to Missouri. I called colleagues and friends who worked for senators and House members. I left voicemails. I sent emails. In short, I was a complete pain in the ass. I knew I had made some traction when, two days later, I received a call from a secretary in the White House asking me to hold the line. I waited for a few moments before getting patched through to a male voice.

"Jen, this is Coddy Johnson from the White House."

Coddy? I hoped I'd heard the name correctly. Wasn't Coddy a woman's name? I charged ahead anyway.

"Hi, Coddy! I'm glad to hear from you."

"Right," he said, brushing off my friendly tone. "Have you been making calls around DC, asking for help with political visits?"

"Yes." I felt proud of my ingenuity.

"Well, that's your first mistake, and you've made a few. You can't do that."

Coddy launched into a tirade about all the ways that I had violated protocol. Which protocols, I didn't know, and as I listened, I experienced a moment of stark clarity. If this had happened to me a few months before, when I was still working on Capitol Hill, Coddy's rebuke would have mortified me. Now, I was only pissed off by White House officials being mad. I couldn't care less what Coddy thought of me.

Coddy kept talking, and my bravado grew. I became defiant. What the hell kind of name was Coddy, anyway?

I stopped him mid-sentence. "Coddy? It is Coddy, isn't it? Look, I need help getting your boss here. You know, *the President of the United States*." I said this as condescendingly as possible, and as if he needed to be reminded who his boss was. "I'm not sure what it is *you* want, but I know President Bush wants Jim to win. Please help us do that."

Through the phone, I heard Coddy laugh, and not in solidarity.

"Okay, look," I huffed. "You sound like a smart guy, Coddy." I was channeling General Schwarzkopf, and no one was more surprised than I was to hear the smartass snark emanating from my own lips. "But the longer it takes, the more money our opponent, Senator Jean Carnahan, will be raising, and the further behind we will be."

Coddy started laughing again. "Okay, Chief," he said, and by his dismissive tone, I was fully aware that he did not consider me to be the chief of anything. "Just stop with the random calls."

He hung up without giving me his phone number, email address, or a time when he would call back. Once the call ended, humiliation crept in. I put my head on my desk. My humiliation took on a new low an hour later when I learned from one of my DC friends that Coddy was not only President Bush's associate political director but also his godson. Collister Johnson III, the man nicknamed Coddy, was the son of the president's best friend. I ran down the hall and dry-heaved into the campaign office toilet, turning on the water in the sink so no one would hear me. I felt sick knowing I had single-handedly screwed up everything. I didn't sleep at all that night.

But the next afternoon, Coddy called me back.

"Hey, Chief." Coddy's tone was breezy, as if nothing had happened the day before. "Let's talk names and dates. When do you want the president to come, and who else can we send that would help Jim?"

Hands trembling, I looked up at the Rand McNally map pinned to the wall of my campaign office. I tried to relax. Crossing my ankles on top of my desk, I looked down at my favorite boots, the high-heeled gold-and-black snakeskin pair, one resting on top of the other. These boots made me feel like a rock star, even if Lloyd hated them. I'd worn them to our first meeting, at Denny's, when he'd condescendingly asked if I planned to wear them through the Missouri farmlands. Now, I wore them as often as I could, sending a subtle message: *I am my own woman, and I'm not scared of anyone*—although, in truth, I was.

CHAPTER 4

Truths

HALLOWEEN AFTERNOON

October 31, 2001 (Age 30)

My flight landed at Washington National Airport on Halloween. Jim's first Washington, DC, fundraiser was that evening, and every member of the campaign team was on pins and needles. The fundraiser would be a critical bellwether for how much excitement and financial support existed to propel Jim's campaign.

I drove the rental car to my house on the Chesapeake Bay. The house was silent as I wheeled my overnight bag through our combination foyer/dining room, and the sound echoed. I heard footsteps on the wood floor in the hall before John appeared, and I set my handbag on the table.

John stepped into the foyer. "We need to talk. Right now."

"John, I can't talk right now. Jim's fundraiser starts in just a few hours, and it will take me an hour to get there. We'll have all weekend to talk."

I still wore the black blazer, jeans, and stiletto boots I'd had on during the flight, and my feet were killing me. I leaned against the table to unzip my boots, one at a time.

"This cannot wait." Walking toward the living room, John motioned to me to follow. "Please."

There was no time for conversation, but I felt unsettled. John's aggressive tone was disconcerting. Twenty minutes. That's what I would give him for this conversation. I looked at my watch.

I walked behind him into our living room. John stood, waiting for me to choose a chair, and when I sat down, he selected one across from me.

"Jen." He said my name but then stopped. I looked down at my watch for dramatic effect.

"Jen," he started again. "I don't know how to tell you this." He paused again and rubbed his forehead. "I need to make a clean start. We need to begin again. I've been having an affair—er, *affairs*. For a long time."

I stared at him.

"I'm really sorry. Really sorry." He was crying now. "But if you agree to come home and have kids, I will stop."

Detachment is an unusual sensation. I'd never experienced it before, but I felt it now. Floating above my body on the ceiling, I looked down at our living room. I saw the woodstove, my books, and the view from our windows out onto the bay. I watched John and me, sitting in our opposite chairs. There was no anger as I floated; I felt nothing. Was it normal to feel nothing? Shouldn't I start crying or screaming?

When I returned to occupy the space inside my body, John was on the floor, on his hands and knees, sobbing. I looked down at him.

"Please say something!"

"Get out of the house." My steadiness surprised me.

"No, Jen. No! Please, let's talk about this."

For years, I had carefully constructed an image of perfection. *Perfect*, sophisticated political lawyer. *Perfect*, wealthy, aspirational young woman. *Perfect*, moral wife with a husband who adored her. In maintaining my image of perfection, I had shut down my own feelings and desires. I'd known I didn't love John from the beginning of our relationship. But marrying him allowed me to escape my father's strict and tyrannical rules and fake my way through a loveless, unsatisfying marriage. It infuriated me that this realization hit me all at once.

John's eyes were red from crying. He got up from the floor and looked confused, unsure of what to do next. I pointed toward the door, and he walked out of the house. I calmly locked it behind him. I quickly threw on my black suit and heels, and as I re-strapped my watch to my wrist, I noticed it was 5:45 p.m. I was going to be late to Jim's fundraiser. I pulled my suitcase back across the house until I reached the foyer, where I stopped. My eyes skipped quickly around the room and out onto the bay. I drew in a deep breath, and then I moved on.

Out of the corner of my eye, I saw John on the lawn as I opened the front door. A sense of alarm pricked throughout my body. Despite his confession, I knew beyond a shadow of a doubt that he loved me deeply and had used these affairs to spur me into loving him back. Once I left our house, John would lose any hold he had over me.

As I closed the front door, John rushed toward me. Instinctively, I picked up the orange plastic jack-o'-lantern from the top of the landing. It was filled to the brim with mini Snickers, Whoppers, and Almond Joy candy bars for the evening's trick-or treaters. With all my strength, I heaved it at him. I watched the orange plastic sail through the air, as if it were moving in slow motion, until it landed, hitting him dead in the face. I took off running, my suitcase barely touching the ground as it bumped along behind me. I heaved my bag and then myself into the rental car before pressing the lock button.

John stood motionless on the lawn, his feet in a sea of tiny candy bars. He stood with one hand holding the jack-o'-lantern and the other in the pocket of his pants as he stared at me, defeated. I slowly pulled the rental car out of the driveway before taking off down the road. I left him standing in the middle of the yard. I would never see my house again.

HALLOWEEN NIGHT

October 31, 2001 (Age 30)

Driving to La Colline, a restaurant on Capitol Hill, would take me an hour in rush hour traffic. As I passed Andrews Air Force Base on the highway, headlights from oncoming cars washed out my skin tone inside my dark car, making me look like a ghost in my rearview mirror. Gradually, my heart stopped pounding. A blanket of deep sadness took the place of my racing mind. I grieved for all the wasted years with John and even felt empathy for him. John knew I didn't love him, and that must have been a terrible burden. I was amazed by how quickly I'd arrived at a place of forgiveness for what he had done, and I realized I had been grieving our marriage from almost the beginning. For years, I hadn't loved John—I had only wanted to love him, and that was a very poor substitute for authentic love.

Miraculously, I found a parking spot close to La Colline and walked inside. Two gold chandeliers illuminated the space, which had bars at either end of the room and a long table of food off to the side. There were so many people that I could barely move through the doorway. Jim stood across the room talking to a senator and two donors. Seeing him returned me to myself; Work Jen was restored. Jim looked over at me and nodded. I smiled back at him.

As the fundraiser came to an end, Jim and I moved to the table at the farthest edge of the room, and I told him about John.

"I'll be praying for you tonight, Jen. Call me tomorrow, okay?"

"Thank you, Jim. Congratulations. I'm going to drive to my parents' house and fly back to St. Louis tomorrow. I'll see you soon."

Bone-tired and emotionally spent, I drove off, due south on I-95 toward Richmond. John and I divorced six months later.

CHRISTMAS

2001 (Age 30)

I woke on Christmas morning with my face so close to my bedroom window that I could feel the rush of cold air when the wind blew against it, rattling the glass. My eyes adjusted slowly to the natural light pushing through the plastic blinds that made a train track of sunlight across my ceiling. I extended my right leg up into the air and turned the clear plastic rod with my toes to open them. The bright winter light poured in. A small sliver of frost glistened at the bottom corner of the glass, like the wing of a snowflake. I traced it with my finger before refocusing my eyes on the view beyond.

The normal commotion of the apartment parking lot was absent today. No car doors opened and closed, no vehicles raced through the complex, no car alarms beeped from accidental detonation. The lot was empty except for a few vehicles, including the new made-in-Missouri Ford Explorer I'd recently rented and my Saab, now covered in brown canvas.

My apartment complex sat on busy Olive Boulevard, a convenient three miles west of the building that would soon become our campaign headquarters. But the apartment itself was depressing and sterile. Its two uninspired square rooms looked out onto the blacktop of the parking lot, and only one skinny tree stood beyond my windows. Without leaves, its spidery branches were barely noticeable. I had no furniture other than a twin-sized bed, a small couch, and a folding table that served as a combination desk and dining room table.

The campaign office had closed for the week of Christmas, but I took advantage of the quiet and worked through the week, including on Christmas Eve. I was in my office when my phone rang. It was Jim, demanding that I join his family for Christmas Eve dinner.

"I'm not going to take no for an answer, Jen."

"Paying me to run your campaign does not involve leaving early." It was a line I said to Jim often, and I knew it sounded particularly ridiculous today.

"Heavens to Pete, it's Christmas Eve! Dinner is at 6:00. We'll see you at 5:00."

I stopped at three different 7-Elevens to collect enough fresh flowers from the cashier countertops to make an acceptable bouquet for Brenda and buy a few card games, stuffed animals, and candy for the Talents' three kids, Michael, Kate, and Chrissy. Chrissy, the youngest at age five, idolized me, and when I rang the doorbell just after five o'clock, I heard her little footsteps bounding across the floor. Jim was standing behind her when the door opened, and she yelled, "Hey, everybody! Miss Blueberry is here!" Then she looped her fingers through mine and guided me to the family room. Four rounds of Uno ensued, all of which I lost, before we took our seats around the dining room table.

Jim spoke first. In the low light of the dining room, the candlelight added a wistfulness to Jim's grace. Wearing his bright red sweater, he looked younger than his forty-six years. He stood behind his chair at the far end of the table.

"We thank you, God, for our blessings on Christmas," he started. "May we always be grateful for one another." He looked around the dining room, his eyes landing on each of us. "My life has been enriched beyond measure by the people at this table. I pray for so many things, God, and I struggle in the waiting. It is difficult for me to hold on to strength and patience. God knows—and everyone at this table knows—that I am not always easy to live with when I am nervous about the future. But I am trying, Lord. I feel you have called me to this Senate race, and I am doing my best. May each of us try the best we can to follow your path and find new blessings this year."

I looked at him and smiled. As Jim was finishing up his grace, he threw in one more blessing for good measure.

"And to Jen. She is a part of this family, and may she always know we are here for her."

While everyone was still quiet, Chrissy stuck out her tongue at me from across the table and started laughing.

"Chrissy!" Brenda snapped, and Chrissy quickly put her tongue back in her mouth. When no one else was looking, I stuck out my own tongue, and Chrissy erupted in giggles. All eyes turned to Chrissy, then to me. Because I, too, had been caught misbehaving, I sheepishly said, "Sorry, Brenda," which made Jim and Kate start to laugh. Quiet, shy Michael, who always seemed much older than his age, rolled his eyes at both of us.

"I think Miss Blueberry needs a glass of wine," Jim said, reaching for the bottle. I felt grateful to be surrounded by people whom I loved and who loved me. I also felt utterly alone.

CHAPTER 5

Gravity

SHINING CITY ON A HILL

January–February 2002 (Age 30)

The first time I officially walked into our new Jim Talent for Senate headquarters, it was so early the sun had not come up yet. I unlocked the front door and stood inside the glass lobby in silence, listening to the hum of the copier. I felt like a trespasser.

The space was very unattractive. On the basement level of an old office building, the rooms resembled a cave dwelling far more than a Shining City on a Hill. But the rent was cheap, and the building's proximity to Olive Boulevard and the narrow, adjacent neighborhood streets made it a difficult spot for opponents to gather and protest outside the headquarters. This made it a highly desirable location, and Lloyd and I decided we would make it work. We desperately needed more people, but to hire more staff, we also needed more room. Five months in, the six staff members who'd started alongside us were running ragged. We needed help.

Inside the four walls of my own office, I created a desk by pushing together three rectangular tables, and an overstuffed tan-and-black love seat sat under the windows. Maps of Missouri covered the entire wall, including the four-by-four-foot Rand McNally, whose surface was now obscured with hundreds of brightly colored pushpins, each indicating one of Jim's stops along the campaign trail. In the past four months, he had visited every one of Missouri's 114 counties and had been to several cities multiple times, including Springfield, Joplin, Kansas City, St. Charles, and Cape Girardeau.

For three months, I'd been calling Coddy every day to ask when the president was coming to Missouri to campaign for Jim, and he'd been putting me off. By February, Lloyd had reached full panic mode. Day after day, I waited, until, at last, the call came.

"Happy Valentine's, Chief. You ready for your present?"

"You tell me. Is it something I want?"

"Yes, I think so."

"Okay, hit me."

"President Bush is coming to St. Louis on March 18 for a fundraising dinner with Jim." Coddy said this so casually that I wasn't sure I'd heard him right.

"Oh my God, Coddy! Really?"

"Yep."

"That's amazing!"

"Yep, I'm pretty awesome."

I started laughing. "Yes, you truly are. Thank you, Coddy. Thank you."

"You've earned it, Chief. I'll call you next week to discuss the details."

I ran into Lloyd's office and opened his door without knocking. "Come into my office right now!" Next, I circled the office to corral Miriam, Brett, and Rich.

When they were all assembled inside my office, Lloyd slapped his knees with the palms of his hands. "Whatever you got to tell us this morning, I sure as shit hope it's good news." Miriam was on the edge of my love seat, next to Lloyd. She wasn't so much sitting as crouching, ready to pounce. Rich and Brett sat in folding chairs across from her. They looked at me expectantly.

"We got W.," I said slowly, referring to President George W. Bush. "He's coming to St. Louis on March 18."

My colleagues erupted into cheers of euphoria. Rich and Brett high-fived, and Miriam looked into the air and shook her hands. "Praise God!" she said, like she was in church. Lloyd breathed a sigh of relief with so much exaggeration that everyone stopped cheering.

"Well, I'll say, Miss Jen. You did it. I always had faith in you. This is just what we needed to get our motors running today, and damn if I ain't grinnin' like a opossum eatin' a sweet potato."

All of us turned to look at Lloyd, and then each other, before we started laughing so hard we were doubled over and clutching our stomachs. Relief is like that, and no one felt it more than I did.

GULL ISLAND

Summer 1985 (Age 13)

From the shoreline of Lake Michigan, where I went to camp for eight summers, you could easily see a small island a few miles out in the Grand Traverse Bay. Its name was Gull Island, and it was known as a place of terrifying legend. On one side of the island, dilapidated remains of a wooden two-story house still stood. White sandy beaches surrounded the tiny, uninhabited drop of land, and what looked to be a giant palm tree—an impossibility in the cold climes of Northern Michigan—added to its mystery.

The older girls told us horror stories around the campfire about the haunted history of Gull Island. Some stories included possessed birds, like in the eponymous movie. Other tales detailed the wealthy and reclusive family who had lived in the house until they were chased away by . . . no one knew for sure, but the girls always filled in the blanks with sinister plotlines and terrifying endings. We routinely passed Gull Island in water-ski boats and on sailboats, but I never wanted to get too close.

As a teenager, I finally gathered enough courage to go to Gull Island. As our water-ski boat slowly inched toward its shore, I peered with one eye open from behind my sunglasses, almost too scared to look. When the boat reached the beach, I was so shocked by what I saw that it took me days to recover. The island was revolting, and not in the creepy, horror-story way. Every foot of the beach was covered in squawking birds—there were thousands of them—large piles of dirty white feathers, and smelly bird droppings. The house was not a house at all but the remains of a boring research station with no palm tree in sight. The truth devastated me, and I never returned.

The mysterious Gull Island had been reduced to its reality: a place covered in feathers and shit.

MONICA LEWINSKY

December 1998 (Age 27)

When the House of Representatives impeached President Bill Clinton in December 1998 for lying under oath about his affair with Monica Lewinsky, I was working as a young lawyer on Capitol Hill. The photograph of Monica wearing a black beret had been circling in the national news for a year.

I've never met Monica Lewinsky. She and I didn't share anything in common as far as I knew, other than being the same age, having a similar hair color, and working for male politicians in DC. But in 1998, not one week went by without me being the butt of some lewd and demeaning comment comparing me to her. That was when I first realized the almost total control men had over women because they had all the power, and I could scarcely dream of things being any different. I personally did not know of even one woman who served as a chief of staff in Congress. No doubt, these realities helped drive me forward to achieve success even though I didn't recognize their influence at the time.

One month before the Bill Clinton–Monica Lewinsky story broke, I'd purchased a black wool beret from the Benetton store in Georgetown and wore it all the time, throwing it on over my mid-length dark brown hair with black sunglasses and bright lipstick. Apparently, Monica had the same idea. After the media plastered the beret photo in outlets across the world, every man I knew—including my own father, on multiple occasions—offered me the unsolicited advice that I should not wear "that hat" again.

Working as a lawyer in Congress, I was widely considered by my colleagues to have the thickest skin of any professional, including men. "A man in women's clothing" was how my closest work friend and onetime boss, Harry, referred to me. I made sure nothing appeared to rattle me on the outside. But the jokes comparing me to Monica were constant, relentless, and disgusting. Some man or other—and it was always a man—would ask me if I liked working "under" my boss, whether I had gotten my job based on my good internship work, or if I liked "to play" with cigars. Many times, I was asked if I liked "to kneel on the job." Men typically made these comments during important work meetings, amplifying the humiliation.

One afternoon, I received a phone call from a senior staff member in the Senate inquiring about a piece of Jim's legislation. He invited me to attend a business lunch with him and other important political colleagues at the Marriott in downtown Washington, DC, and I excitedly accepted, thinking the lunch would be an opportunity to make new connections. The eight of us sat at a round table, all men but me. As we ate, I accidentally spilled a drop of ranch dressing on my dress. From across the table, a man I'd never met asked me if I was going to wash my dress or keep it dirty "with the stain as a memento, like Monica." All the men laughed uproariously at the joke, including my Senate colleague.

Burning with embarrassment and rage, I stood up from the table and threw my napkin onto my plate. I did not take even a moment's pause. "I've heard about your impotence," I sneered, staring down at the jokester. All laughing instantly stopped, and seven sets of eyes were upon me. "I'm sure your own inability to get it up is what makes you tell crude jokes about women."

I turned and left the table. Just like every other time I've defended myself in this way, I did not look back at the offenders, feeling the silence of their dropped jaws on my back. I walked down the hall at a speed bordering on a run and went into the bathroom, where I sat on a toilet seat inside a stall, fully clothed, and sobbed in silence.

The truth is that most gold-covered paths leading to the end of a rainbow are actually buried under steaming piles of shit, just like Gull Island. The key is being willing to pick up a shovel. You will use that shovel many times to muck your way through to the rainbow, where you will arrive dirty and sick from the stench.

THE KANSAS CITY STAR

March 2002 (Age 30)

In the two weeks leading up to the President Bush dinner, Steve Kraske, the political journalist at *The Kansas City Star*, called the campaign office with the news that he was working on a story. Kraske's liberal leanings were well-known, and we figured he was being fed a false and negative narrative by the Missouri Democratic Party. We weren't worried at first. But the more Kraske called the office, the more his questions shifted to asking about me. I couldn't figure out his angle.

On Saturday, March 15, three days before the President Bush event in St. Louis, I stood in the arrivals lounge of the St. Louis Lambert Airport waiting to pick up my parents; I'd gotten them tickets to the President Bush dinner. When my phone rang, I pulled it out of my bag and was surprised to see Jim's number on the caller ID.

"Jim?"

"Jen, I just heard from Steve Kraske."

Steve Kraske had just given Jim the heads-up that in tomorrow's most widely read Sunday edition of *The Kansas City Star*, a front-page, two-thousand-word story would run accusing both Jim and me of breaking federal campaign law.

"What?" I yelled in a loud whisper.

Kraske's story alleged that Jim's and my work at the law firm was a sham to cover up Jim's alleged plot to run for the US Senate from the moment we joined the law firm. I was aghast. Later that afternoon, I called Lloyd.

"Facts don't matter," Lloyd said. "The Missouri Democratic Party pitched this story to Kraske, and he bought it hook, line, and sinker."

"Are you being serious?"

"I am freakin' serious, Jen. Serious as a heart attack."

I paused, letting his words sink in.

"What will we do?"

"Our attorneys will file a lawsuit against them."

"On what grounds?"

"Don't know yet, and it doesn't matter." It sounded like Lloyd was rubbing his chin. "The FEC won't get to the case for over a year, and we won't have to prove shit until the campaign is long over."

CLIMBING HIGHER

1984 (Age 13)

Late one night, when I was thirteen years old, my father and I sat together at the kitchen table in our house. He was still dressed in his navy blue Brooks Brothers sports coat and red tie from work. Leaning toward the kitchen cabinets, he pulled a legal pad from the top drawer before reaching into his jacket pocket to remove his silver Cross pen. He twisted the tip and turned toward me, his signal to pay attention.

On the paper, my dad drew a large, upside-down *V*.

"This is a mountain," he said. I nodded in recognition.

My dad drew no trees and no clouds in the sky, but at the bottom of the mountain, he drew a straight line to represent the ground. I leaned over the table to watch him draw.

"You asked me how I know Christian Science is the 'right' religion," he said, repeating my earlier question for effect. "I look at it this way."

He drew a small circle at the pinnacle of the mountaintop.

"This is the top of the mountain, the very highest place. The summit symbolizes the heights we hope we will ascend to, which is the place closest to God. Right here." He tapped the paper twice.

Then he sketched a series of lines traveling up the mountain and stopping at different points. Some were midway up the mountain; others did not reach that high.

"All of us are striving to make it up the mountain, but most of us won't make it. For me, Christian Science is the way to get me all the way to the top." His next line went from the bottom of the mountain straight to the top. "Getting there requires constant discipline and hard work. But if you're always striving, you'll make it to the top, where you know God. *That* is Christian Science."

My dad paused. He looked across the table at me before drawing another vertical line, which suddenly curved before going back down to the ground. "If you stop working and aren't disciplined, you will slide down the mountain."

I did not know if he intended for that line to represent what he perceived as my path, but I was determined to never, ever be that line.

"Stay close to God," he warned. "Work hard and keep working hard. That is how you will get to the summit. That's when you will know who you are, and you will be respected."

PRESIDENT BUSH IN ST. LOUIS

March 18, 2002 (Age 30)

What an outsider witnessed at America's Center on the evening of March 18, 2002, at the Jim Talent dinner with President Bush was a perfectly executed event that raised more than a million dollars from the hundreds of people in the ballroom. The dinner's speeches inspired five standing ovations in support of Jim and the president. From my perch on the platform by the TV cameras, I looked like the most important woman in politics on the proudest night of my professional life.

But that is not what I felt. For three days, I'd dealt with the fallout of the Kraske article, which was precisely what he had intended with its timing. I had not slept or eaten. My parents had barely laid eyes on me since arriving in St. Louis, and they were angry with me. As I watched the dinner unfold from the top of the platform, my overwhelming sensation was not exhilaration but guilt and shame. I became a little girl again, a girl who had been so bad this time that she was unable to make it up the mountain to see God, and she'd also been slandered on the front page of *The Kansas City Star*. Even worse, I'd been too weak to put my fears aside and give my parents the attention they deserved. There I was, surrounded by some of the most important people on the planet, who were in that ballroom because of my work, and I couldn't get over my sadness and anger. I was furious at myself for feeling this way, which only made me feel more pathetic.

The Monster was back, and she was seething. *You pathetic mess*, she hissed at me, *you will never, ever succeed.*

When I got back to my apartment late that night, my parents were already asleep on the queen blow-up bed in my living room. They left before dawn the next morning. My dad had volunteered to drive my Saab back to Virginia for safekeeping, and they wanted to get an early start. I heard them packing up to leave at 5:00 a.m. for the twelve-hour drive ahead of them, but I pretended I was sleeping. I did not want to have any more conversations or hear about how I'd let them down. I let them leave without saying goodbye.

CHAPTER 6

Becoming Unwired

PARALYZED

October 2021 (Age 50)

One morning, when I'd lived in California for almost a year, I rolled over in bed and discovered I couldn't move my neck without experiencing terrible pain. I'd slept strangely on my neck many times before, resulting in stiffness, but this morning's pain was on a whole new level. It was so bad I could barely think.

One quickly learns a secret about the fastest way to resolve problems in Southern California: The key to health and happiness is not found at the doctor's office but with one's hairdresser. I immediately dialed his cell phone.

"Todd? Todd, it's Jen. I don't know what to do. My neck—it's on fire."

"Fire hot or fire agony?"

"Fire agony."

"Got it. Hold on and await my instructions." I could almost hear the James Bond theme music as Todd channeled M, the chief of the British Secret Intelligence Service.

I didn't need to wait long. By midmorning, Todd had gotten

me an appointment with John, the owner of Redlands Massage Therapy. When I arrived, I expected the place to be a variation of the corporate wellness chain Massage Envy, with its shiny white shelves showcasing expensive skin products and a menu of modern self-care services, but nothing could have been further from the truth. As I held the door open for a man who had hair down to his waist and wore orange corduroy culottes, I walked inside and realized Redlands Massage Therapy was a bohemian paradise where people clearly smoked a gargantuan amount of weed. Crystals glimmered from every surface, dreamcatchers dangled from the ceiling, and essential oils burned in Indonesian-style atomizers.

I wondered whether I should sit down or run. I compromised and remained standing, concentrating on my throbbing neck. Within moments, John appeared. I don't know what I'd expected him to be like, but by now, my expectations had gone out the window. John was bald, significantly shorter than me, and wore no shoes or socks. His faded yellow T-shirt promoted a surf shack in Hawaii, and I could barely make out the faded gray lettering that exclaimed, *Some like it Hot*.

"Jen? I'm John. What brings you in today?"

"Thanks for fitting me into your tight schedule." Todd had emphasized that getting an appointment had not been easy. "My neck is killing me. I can't move it without excruciating pain."

"Accident? Stress? Do you know?"

"No. I just woke up and it was like this."

"Have you been to see an intuitive therapist before?"

Before? I didn't know I was seeing one now. What the hell was he talking about?

"Um, no."

"Okay. Well, why don't we get started? Take off all your clothes and lie face up under this sheet. I'll be back in a few minutes."

As I slowly undressed, I looked around the room. Shelves of books by Eckhart Tolle, Michael Singer, and Bessel van der Kolk lined the studio walls, and John had artificial (I hoped) skeletons resting on his countertops. Medical posters, landscape paintings, and unusual objects hung on his walls. Once I was completely naked, I scooted under the green flannel sheet and waited for John to return.

As soon as he walked back into the room, he got straight to work. I have had many massages in my life, and what John did to my body was not a massage. It started off normally enough; John rubbed my shoulders and massaged my arms. But when he got to my right hand, he stopped. "What happened here?"

"I don't know what you mean."

"Has anything ever happened to your right hand?"

"Um . . . well, yes. To my thumb. But that was twenty years ago."

He did not press me for details, and I did not give them. By the time he got to my ribcage, he was clearly quite concerned.

"Turn over," he instructed, and I obeyed. He hopped up onto the table and, on all fours, started rubbing my upper back with such force I thought he was going to break my spine. It hurt more than my neck did. Then, John started grunting. The force of him pressing his hands deep into the sinews of my back muscles caused him to utter sounds like those made by a professional tennis player giving the racket swing their very all. My horror at the situation evolved into a feeling of ridiculousness, and I stifled a laugh.

When I turned over again to face upward, John stood next to me and lightly put both of his hands on my skin, above my ribcage on the right side. Suddenly, a flood of emotions rushed to the surface of my body and mind. A minute earlier, I had been laughing—in pain, but laughing—and now, tears inexplicably began pouring down my cheeks. They ran down my neck and into my hair. I had no idea what was happening. What I felt was a bright sadness. The tears were from a place inside me that was terribly distraught and unhappy, but it was as if I'd been seen for the first time. I felt a stirring, like a premonition that a new, more whole version of myself was ready to emerge.

"Let the tears come," John said. "Do not hold back. You are safe here."

When he finished, he asked me to get dressed and meet him in his tiny office next door. Exhaustion weighed on me like a blanket, and I felt confused. What had happened in John's studio? What had John seen about me? Suddenly, I felt very exposed and embarrassed. I walked into his office a few minutes later with my credit card out, thinking this was the room where I'd make a payment. He asked me to have a seat in the chair across from him.

"I assume you've realized by now that the problem is not with your neck."

That's when it occurred to me that my neck didn't hurt anymore. I was shocked and placed my hand on the back of my neck in disbelief. "No?" I said.

"No. You are holding a lot of trauma in your body. It is concerning."

I stared blankly.

"Your ribs," he said. "Something happened there?"

"Yes," I said.

We stared at one another for several moments.

"Do you see a psychotherapist?"

"No," I responded with a strength of conviction I did not feel. "But I'm willing to come back and see you again. I admit that something unexplainable happened in your studio today, and I do feel a lot better."

His face carried an expression of knowing something I did not. He nodded.

"Let's see what progress we can make together, and we'll reassess in a few months."

BURNED

April 2, 2002 (Age 30)

At the time, I didn't see it as the moment to remember, my moment, the one that would separate me from my former life forever. I had no clue then that I would later identify it as the beginning of the end.

Springfield, Missouri, is the state's third-largest city and the crown jewel for Republicans. It anchors Southwest Missouri, the state's most heavily conservative bastion. A Republican running for Senate in Missouri must dominate there by an overwhelming margin to win statewide. It was our most frequent campaign stop, and on April 3, the campaign was hosting a lunch with Jim and more than three hundred Republican women at the original Bass Pro Shops. On the day before the event, April 2, every woman in our St. Louis campaign office prepared to embark on the four-hour, cross-state trip to Springfield.

Miriam's car was already in the parking lot when I arrived at the campaign headquarters that morning. Surprisingly, so was Lloyd's. I walked inside and made a beeline for Lloyd's office. Through the door, I heard him talking loudly on the phone. Not five minutes later, Lloyd walked into my office and closed the door behind him.

"I've just gotten off the phone with Jim," Lloyd said in an exasperated tone. "He and Brenda are concerned about the campaign's public fundraising report due this week."

During an election year, the federal government requires

US Senate campaigns to submit quarterly reports tracking the money they've raised and spent, which they publish on a publicly accessible website. The media then writes stories about who is ahead in the money race—a sign of which candidates have political momentum. In the wake of the Kraske fiasco, the article accusing me of breaking campaign finance law, Jim and Brenda were more concerned than ever about Jean Carnahan raising more money than we did.

"I know you're headed to Springfield and don't have time for this bullshit. But, Jen, I don't either. I'm not even an official part of this campaign."

"You're in the thick of it with us now, Lloyd. Like it or not."

"I'll help you—yes, ma'am, I will. But dealing with candidate bullshit ain't my forte, which means it ain't my problem."

"Understood, Lloyd. I'll call Jim and Brenda on my drive to Springfield."

Miriam left the campaign headquarters first, and I promised that I would leave right behind her. I watched her drive away as I jotted down my talking points for calling Jim and Brenda. When I finished, I threw my computer bag into my Ford Explorer and pulled out of our campaign headquarters. It was midmorning.

The day was gray and thick with low clouds. Soybean and corn farms, still barren from winter, replaced the city landscape as I traveled further from St. Louis on I-44. An hour west, I neared the city of Sullivan, where the rolling hills met the Meramec River. Occasional walls of limestone lined the highway—teasers for the miles of spectacular caves below the ground. The outlaw Jesse James and his band of men hid in these caves in the 1870s, and the exit for Missouri's popular tourist attraction was a few miles ahead. As I drove, I mentally prepared to call Jim and Brenda about our campaign finance report, knowing they were going to be panicky and I needed to remain calm. I took deep breaths.

I looked across at the passenger seat of my Ford Explorer. I'd taken off my high-heeled gold-and-black snakeskin boots before setting out, and they sat next to my Blackberry on the seat beside me. Seeing the boots made me think of Lloyd, and I laughed. He hated those boots, but that didn't stop me from wearing them. Lloyd may have won when it came to getting rid of my Saab, but he would never win when it came to my shoes.

I rolled down my window to breathe in the cold, and I released my breath slowly. The air whipped around my face. My long hair thrashed the back of my driver's seat and the ceiling of the car. I looked over again at my passenger seat and something in the side-view mirror caught my eye: The reflection of a tractor trailer's front grill and a male driver at the wheel was so near that it startled me. The semi got closer. Then closer.

I screamed at the impact. Time paused and that was the last time I thought about the campaign—and my life—as I had before.

The semi hit the back of my Ford Explorer with a force so jarring that my car took off into the air. Under me, over me, and around me, there was only air until my car began to somersault. I hit the ground upside down, and the metal of my roof smashed into the pavement. The sound of the impact detonated like a bomb. *BOOM!* My car lifted again. Each second held suspense, and I did not think I would survive. I waited. I counted. One, two, three, four. *BOOM!* I knew this was how I would die.

I was certain I was dead when I heard the singing. Soft and low, the voice was both faraway and all around me. "O Gentle Presence," the same hymn my brother and I had heard in my dad's car when I was nine. I listened, and just like it had twenty-one years earlier, the voice sounded real, as if someone were singing in the seat beside me. It drowned out the noises of rolling and crashing steel. I felt calm but separated from my own body, and I watched myself roll.

When the singing stopped, everything was quiet. I willed myself to open my eyes. Slowly, weight returned to my body and my surroundings came back into focus. When I wiggled my arms and legs, they moved. I touched my stomach with my fingers and rested them there, feeling my belly rise and fall with my breath. I ran my fingers over my chin, mouth, nose, and eyes. I looked at my fingertips. No blood.

The car had come to rest with the passenger side straight up in the air and the driver's side pressed to the ground. My window was still open, and my face hovered so close to the earth that I could smell the damp grass. The windshield resembled the crackled surface of a dry desert, with jagged veins of shattered glass running its full length. I could not see outside the car. The roof had collapsed, concave down to the seats. Only around my body was the ceiling still intact, giving me the sensation of sitting inside a bubble of twisted steel. I was trapped, but I was alive.

From a place beyond the car's pedals, my feet began to feel warm, then hot. I smelled smoke. I felt locked in slow motion, muddled about what to do next. My brain moved like molasses, skipping between thoughts like a stone on the surface of the water. *How will I get out? Where am I? Are those orange flames coming from my engine?*

Then, my car began to lift off the ground. Once I was righted, my eyes became level with a man's face, inches from my own. He was leaning into my open window.

"Are you hurt?"

"I . . . I don't think so." I was blinking at him, my speech jumbled. He spoke with urgency.

"I'm a firefighter, and I'm here to help you. We can't open your car door." The man did not avert his eyes from mine. "You're going to have to slide out of the window. Can you do that? I'll help you."

He reached inside my window to unbuckle my seat belt and pull me out. I hit the ground with a thud. When I looked up, the highway was gridlocked in both directions. I knelt in the soft ground of the embankment. An ambulance was parked several feet away in the grass.

"Can you walk?"

I nodded.

We staggered together, passing one of my snakeskin boots lying in the mud off to the side. Two EMTs helped me climb into the ambulance.

"We expected to pull a corpse from that car," the taller of the two said.

I nodded again. I found it difficult to speak.

They wrapped me in heavy blankets, and I looked out of the back of the ambulance. Lights flickered, and voices came and went. I watched firefighters blast water at my car. My Ford Explorer was no longer recognizable, and I had to look away.

I thought of Miriam driving to Springfield about thirty miles ahead of me. Her luggage and all the event supplies were in the back of my Ford Explorer. The very same moment this realization dawned on me, it occurred to me that I did not care about any of it.

"Ma'am? Ma'am?"

I looked up from my bench inside the ambulance and realized my ears were ringing. An EMT stood above me holding my melted Blackberry, the thin black case singed and misshapen at the bottom. "We found this in the grass." I took it from him and pressed a button. The screen lit up. I dialed the campaign office and heard the phone ring.

Our intern's cheerful voice answered the phone.

"Hello! Talent for Senate!"

I was having difficulty speaking, and the words were jumbled as they escaped from my lips.

"It's Jen. Rich. Rich. I need him."

"One moment, Jen."

The instrumental version of "Copacabana" played in the background until Rich picked up the phone.

"Hiya, Jen."

"Rich, I've been in an accident. I need help."

"Oh my god, Jen. Are you okay? Where are you?"

I looked up at the EMT, who anticipated my question. "You're going to Sullivan County Memorial Hospital."

"Sullivan County Memorial Hospital," I repeated.

"Got it. We'll be there. Is there anything you need?"

"My accident is on the radio. With my name. The firefighters are listening to it on the news right now."

"Okay, Jen, I'll take care of it. We'll be there soon."

After I hung up, I lowered the phone to my lap and looked down at myself. Mud cakes had formed on my feet, and a yellow liquid I didn't recognize stained my black pants. I tried picking at it with my fingernail until a strange sensation washed over me. My limbs felt paralyzed before my entire body began convulsing. I tried pressing my hands together to steady them. I massaged one with the other, but nothing stopped the violent shaking. That's when the sound came. Both a moan and a cry, it spilled from my mouth, but it did not originate there. It rose from a place in my stomach and seeped through the pores of my skin. Deep and guttural, the sound seemed to have no ending. Even my embarrassment could not stop it.

The EMT put his hand on my shoulder. "It's shock," he said. "You can't stop it from coming, but hang in there. You'll be fine." But I wasn't fine.

That very moment is suspended in time as the one when my life began to change. An awareness hit me, an experience that, I later learned, happens to people who are snatched from the jaws of death. I had been given a second chance. Why I, of all people, had been spared from dying, I did not know, but I felt utterly unworthy. For the first time in my adult life, clarity pierced my entire being. I realized I did not authentically believe in anything I was doing. I did not care about Republican politics or the United States Senate or even whether Jim Talent won the campaign. I knew this deep inside my bones, and the shame of my inauthentic lie of a life overwhelmed me.

All the way to the hospital, I pinned my gaze to the floor and cried.

RIBBONS OF SUNSHINE

April 2002 (Age 30)

The next morning, the pain pulsed through my body like lightning. My bones felt as if they had been crushed, stepped on, and ground into pulverized dust. I kept touching my ribs, certain they must be poking through my skin. Breathing took enormous effort. I could not do it without concentration because the pain was too intense.

I found relief only by lying flat on the floor. I stretched my body across the carpet so I resembled a corpse with my arms hanging by my sides. Hour after hour, I stared up at the ceiling. I wanted to cry, but every time I tried, I couldn't find the tears. I begged God for help. My tattered leather Bible lay next to me on the carpet. I wanted to find inspiration in the words, but they meant nothing to me. Both my Bible and I were turned toward the sky, waiting for God to transform us back into something recognizable. But God did not come.

A bottle of orange painkillers sat on my kitchen counter. I could see them from almost everywhere in my apartment, but I did not take them.

At the very same time, a new thought began rising inside me. Alone in my apartment day after day, I felt a tiny and teetering sense of confidence. *Hang on*, my insides whispered. *It's coming.* The message was hard to trust given the horrifying evidence all around me, but there was something in it that I believed.

On the third day after the accident, I was lying on my living room floor in the path of sunshine streaming through the glass of the living room patio doors when I heard a knock at the front door. I managed to slide across the carpet and open the door; a large bouquet of flowers sat on the landing. I opened the card.

> *Jen, we are thinking of you and wishing you a very speedy recovery. You are awesome and we need you!*
> *—Your Friends at The White House*

I didn't call Coddy for six days.

A thought began to crystallize in my mind, and I wondered at it for some time. Lying in the ribbons of sunshine on my carpeted floor, it occurred to me that maybe God had been speaking to me all along, but I hadn't understood the message because the language had changed.

SUPERPOWERS

Mid-April 2002 (Age 30)

On Monday morning, seven days after my accident, Miriam picked me up at my apartment. She helped me down the stairs, my arm draped over her shoulders. When I arrived in the office, the Talent for Senate campaign staff came into the lobby and clapped and cheered my arrival. I put on my biggest, fakest smile and waved.

Sitting in my office, I waited for my driven, hard-charging self to return. This did not happen. I tried to concentrate on memos, briefings, and meetings, but I could not reclaim my passion or my singular focus. My intensity, always one of my superpowers, was gone.

My phone rang and I jumped. Our campaign airplane pilot, Mike, was on the other end of the line.

"Did Jim tell you that my wife and I were stuck in the westbound traffic backup your car accident caused on Interstate 44?" Mike said this almost in a whisper.

"No, Mike. I didn't know."

"I heard on the radio that it was you who was in that accident, and we started praying. It looked so bad, Jen. I was sure you were dead."

I did not know what to say, so I sat motionless in my office chair.

"You know, Jen, sometimes God wants us to listen. You are always running so fast. I think God is trying to tell you that you need to slow down. Maybe you're supposed to hear something new?"

GRACE

May–June 2002 (Age 30)

At thirty, my impressive résumé read like an ancient scroll citing my accomplishments, but my list of "I Have Nevers" might have been even longer. Key among them: I had never been to a bar for an alcoholic drink. Never danced in a nightclub. Never had a romantic fling, and, in the few times I'd had sex, never enjoyed it. I'd enjoyed a glass or two of wine dining out with

Lloyd or at Jim and Brenda's house, but I had never been even slightly drunk. Vodka, gin, or tequila had never touched my lips, and the last time I'd drunk a beer was in high school when my friends and I giggled our way through a few cans of Milwaukee's Best at house parties.

In late May 2002, two months after my car accident, my friend Currie persuaded me to go on a clipper ship cruise in the Caribbean. It was framed as a chance to recuperate and recover. Jim thought it was a fantastic idea and convinced me to go. I brought with me one medium-sized bag full of campaign work and a smaller bag of clothes, intending to work every chance I got. My attempts to coax Old Jen back into existence—the work-intense Jen who had endured the car accident but could come out on the other side as the same person—remained in full force.

On the last Saturday in May, a taxi drove us from the Barbados airport to the Bridgetown seaport. Currie pointed toward the docked sailboat as we turned into the harbor. The 360-foot clipper ship held only 170 passengers and was one of the smaller ships at the dock. But it was by far the most magnificent with its three masts standing tall against the brilliant blue of the Caribbean Sea.

We stood in line to board. On the ship's deck, four men and one woman wearing white uniforms sat at a long table checking passengers' passports, and a man of some authority escorted us down to the far end. I handed my passport to a young man who flipped it open, turned to my photo page, and immediately started to laugh. On the plane to Barbados, I'd joked with Currie that my passport photo would win a prize for having the closest human likeness to a chipmunk. While in real life I was tall and thin, my cheeks were so puffy in the photo that they looked to be holding large stores of nuts in preparation for winter, and my beady eyes peered out from behind my enormous cheeks.

"Nice photo," the man said offhandedly in a British accent, chuckling. He didn't look up at me, but I surmised he was in his twenties. His white seafaring uniform resembled the kind worn by Captain Stubing in the 1980s TV show *The Love Boat*, except that the bright gold tassels on this man's shoulders added extra flair. The tassels looked odd on such a young man.

"Nice uniform," I responded without missing a beat. The man's gaze shot up from my passport to my face. Blond, tan, and gorgeous. He smiled.

Ladies and gentlemen, meet Sam from England.

HEAD OF WATERSPORTS

May–June 2002 (Age 30)

Sam's title on the ship was Head of Watersports. I defined the world and everyone in it by their job titles: chief of staff, political director, legal counsel, legislative assistant. Head of Watersports was new to me. For passengers wanting to scuba dive, snorkel, or water ski, Sam was apparently your guy. I learned this information that night over drinks on the ship's deck when I asked him what a man from the UK knew about water-skiing. Call me crazy, but I don't think of rainy England as a place where people flock so they can learn to slalom.

"I had my own scuba diving business in Thailand, and before that, I lived in Bali. We water-skied there."

Sam's impressive reply only amplified his already-significant swagger, which I found to be equal parts intriguing and annoying. He was catching on to my dismissive tone about his job, and not to be outdone, he lobbed back a question. This guy was really starting to piss me off.

"What do *you* know about water sports?" He pointed his question at me.

I looked at him and paused meaningfully before answering, making space in the conversation to allow my response its appropriate due.

"My dad taught me to water-ski when I was six," I puffed. Then, for good measure, I added, "My parents have a house on a lake, their *second* home, with a championship water-ski boat."

Admittedly, Sam and I had gotten off on the wrong foot, which—I'll own it—was mostly my fault. I felt a split personality growing inside me on the ship's deck. While we sat talking, I caught myself sneaking glances at Sam's tan chest moving under his white uniform, which was now mostly unbuttoned, and his blond curls falling over his ears and down his neck. I looked at his shoulders and arms, and I imagined him reaching over to kiss me, then kissing him back, hard, before pulling his shirt over his head and . . .

I caught myself mid-fantasy, and it absolutely horrified me. My body began stirring in places I didn't even know I had, much less that they could stir on their own. I felt totally out of control. I had traveled all the way to the southernmost parts of the Caribbean to revive Old Jen, not to be charmed by Sam, the Cruise Ship Casanova. I needed to shut down my rogue feelings, and stat. Unfortunately, my body had a mind of its own, a detail I'd never had occasion to experience before. My quick tongue and biting words were the only defenses I had left.

"So, what do you do back in the USA?" Sam turned toward me on his barstool. His green eyes focused intensely on mine. I had to look away as I went in for the kill.

"It's pretty complicated. I don't think you would understand." I said this with a sneer.

I heard myself talking and thought, *What a bitch.* But this realization did not slow me down in the slightest. I watched as his beautiful face hardened, and I knew I had lost him, just as I'd intended.

"I work on a United States Senate campaign—a very important one, actually. If you have any questions about politics, I will try to make my answers easy to understand."

Within a few minutes, Sam and I were no longer talking but yelling at one another. Currie and the others left the table.

"You work for a Republican, Jen, the party of racists and fools who are systematically destroying the planet. I don't know how you can be so smug. I'm done. I do not want to waste my time talking to you anymore." He turned and walked away.

I looked around, embarrassed to be left in the wake of the silence created by his departure. I didn't know what else to do but go back to the stateroom I shared with Currie, alone. I opened the door to my cabin and was surprised that Currie had not returned. I stripped down to my bra and underwear and climbed into my bed without brushing my teeth or even turning on the light. I was fuming, anger rising inside me, and I could not pinpoint the reason. Why was this bothering me so much? Who cared what Sam thought? He was just some random cruise ship employee who was upset at being denied another notch on his bedpost. Thoughts swirled in loops inside my brain when I heard a voice whisper directly and loudly into my left ear.

"Jen," The Voice said. "Drop the chip."

I shot up in bed and turned on the light, stunned. No one was in the room, but I knew what I had heard. Drop the chip? What chip?

For weeks, I had been begging God to send me a message, but this was ridiculous. Was God really choosing *now* to speak? This possibility made me even angrier, and I turned the light off to sit quietly in the darkness. I put my arms around my knees and said out loud to the empty room, "Okay. I'm listening."

It was a thought, not a voice, that came to me next in the form of a question: *Who are you?*

I obediently answered. "I am the soon-to-be chief of staff for—"

"No," The Voice interrupted. "Who *are* you?"

I had no idea what to say. I sat in the blackness and wondered at many things. Mostly, my thoughts landed on how I would feel if I did not have an important political job to define me. It was terrifying. *If not this, who would I be?* And I did not know.

REVELATIONS

May–June 2002 (Age 30)

Bright sunshine poured through the porthole above my bed the next morning. I rolled over and saw Currie sleeping in the bed next to me. I quietly eased out of my covers and slipped into my black string bikini, wrapped a sarong around my waist, and left the room. Above deck, the intense Caribbean sunshine reflected off the sparkling sea. The ship sailed toward Tobago Cays, and the stunning small islands dotting the horizon took my breath away.

The space that had served as a bar last night had been converted into a water-filling station, and as I topped up my water bottle, Sam appeared through the lounge's double doors as if he had been waiting for me. Without saying anything, he handed me a tattered paperback copy of *The French Lieutenant's Woman*, a novel by John Fowles.

"This is my favorite book in the world," he said. "I want you to have it."

In the sunlight, his green eyes were so vibrant that they were almost translucent. I smiled at him.

"I'm sorry, Jen. I behaved like an asshole last night."

"Oh, Sam, no. I'm the one to blame. I'm so sorry."

"I have to go to work now, but I'd like to see you later if that's okay."

My change of heart resulted from The Voice telling me to drop the chip the night before. I cannot account for Sam's change in attitude toward me, other than to say that I don't think divine revelations are ever a one-way street.

Sam smiled before turning to walk toward the stern of the ship. I walked to the forward deck and sat in a lounge chair. Six massive white sails filled the space above me, and beyond them was the endless blue sky. Just ahead, the Tobago Cays came into full view as the ship slowed to a crawl. Rigging from the masts squealed as the sails began to fall. The men were preparing to drop anchor and moor the boat.

I looked down at Sam's copy of *The French Lieutenant's Woman* and ran my fingers over the faded face of the mysterious woman on the cover. I opened its creased pages, and my eyes fell on sixteen words: *There is only one good definition of God: the freedom that allows other freedoms to exist.*

I stretched out my legs on the chair and looked up at the sky before putting my headphones on. I contemplated both the words and the person who had given them to me. I turned up the volume on Sheryl Crow's "Steve McQueen" and I felt like I was flying.

In the afternoon, Sam taught me to scuba dive. I was scared at first, but he told me I could go as slowly as I needed to while my ears popped like they do on an airplane. When my ears finally cleared, we sank deeper. The quiet of the sea was what surprised me the most, and as Sam pointed out coral and fish, a stingray floated by us so close that I could have touched it. I whipped my head around to see if Sam saw it, too. Even behind his mask, I could see his smile. He took my hand and we swam together, kicking with the fins on our feet.

Back on the Tobago Cays later that day, Sam and I leaned our backs against a fallen palm tree and talked. As the sun fell from the sky, Sam asked me if he could have another chance. I looked at the piercing blue of the ocean while letting the white sand roll through my fingers. Of course, he already knew the answer would be yes.

NOTCHES

May–June 2002 (Age 30)

I could not remember the last time I had dressed up to entice a man. I'd recently bought a dress of thin black silk with spaghetti straps, suggesting a kind of sexy I'd never been. But it hugged my curves in that *just-right* way, and I'd reasoned my way into buying it. As I walked into the dining room to meet Sam for dinner, he did not hide his reaction.

Dinner led to drinks on deck. Fellow crew members asked Sam to play his guitar and sing. It surprised me how beautifully he played. I stayed off to the side, watching him. An hour later, when he finished, he held my hand as we walked down the stairs and into his cabin. It looked just like a cozy studio apartment. Books lined the shelves and a small television sat on a table.

He moved across the bed to kiss my bare shoulder and then my mouth before lowering the straps of my dress with his fingers. I moved to him, kissing him hard. We fell into one another with an intensity I did not know existed. He kissed every part of me, his hands beneath me and on my hips, my stomach, my neck. My fingers moved over him in ways I had never touched anyone before. I watched his face as he watched mine. We did not break our gaze.

No natural light entered Sam's interior cabin, and the only illumination came from a tiny blue light next to his bed. That night, I knew when Sam woke up because he would slide his hand around my waist and roll me over to look at him. My broken ribs would hurt so much I would wince, but I never let him know. Our faces would land inches from one another on his pillow, and we could see the outlines of our bodies in the pale light. The curves of my face, the hollow of his neck and chest, the rise of my hip bones. Sam traced my contours with his fingers.

He told me what he saw when he looked at me. Fear, he said, and sadness. It surprised me when he said that.

"Are you sad?" he asked.

"Yes," I replied. "But I can't talk about it yet."

When I woke up the next morning, Sam had on his white uniform with gold tassels. He was leaning over the bed.

"I have to go to my eight a.m. Captain's Meeting now," he whispered. "But tomorrow is my birthday, and I want to celebrate it tonight. Will you celebrate my birthday with me?"

"I will," I said. I reached up and pulled him back into bed.

After his meeting, we spent every moment together for the next two days. Several times, I debated telling him about my car accident, but it felt too intimate, too emotional, too *revealing*. But when Jeff Buckley's title song, "Grace," played through Sam's small cabin speakers for the fourth time in three days, I decided it was time. The lyrics haunted me. It was his favorite song, and it ignited my own memories of waiting, trapped in the fire of my burning car. Sam strummed his guitar along to Buckley's, and when I asked him if I could tell him what it was that made me sad, he nodded and set his guitar on the floor.

Sam sat with his back against his bed frame, and I faced him with my legs lightly wrapped around him. Shirtless, he wore only Thai fishing pants, and I had one of his shirts buttoned loosely across my chest. Recounting the rolling and the crashing, tears poured from my eyes. When I finished talking, Sam said nothing and betrayed nothing, and I had never felt so vulnerable in my life.

Sam reached out his hands and gently placed them on my waist. He slid me to him, so close that our chests touched. His green eyes sliced through me. Resting his face against mine, he did not kiss me. He placed his hands lightly on my skin, above my ribcage.

I gently wrapped my arms around his neck and kissed him. We remained there, in that same position—or very close to it—until the next morning.

An hour before the passengers were required to disembark, Sam walked me back to my stateroom. We traded email addresses and kissed a long kiss that I did not want to end but which I knew must end. Then, I slowly opened the door to find Currie, freshly showered and packing. I sat down on my bed and stared at my unopened computer bag. Since getting off the plane in Barbados, I had not checked my email or done a moment's work.

We climbed into our cab to head to the airport. I turned one last time to look at the ship and its towering masts that reached into the Caribbean sky. I made sure my passport was inside my bag before pulling out *The French Lieutenant's Woman* and beginning to read where I'd left off.

CHAPTER 7

After the Caribbean

THE GOLDEN GODDESS

Early June 2002 (Age 30)

The plane touched down on the tarmac at St. Louis Lambert International Airport around midnight, and my body was sitting in a window seat near the front of the plane. My soul, however, felt like it was somewhere else.

The truest thing I can say about my time in the Caribbean is that some essence of who I am as a woman was revealed to me there, and upon returning home, I felt like I was collapsing back into a mere shell. Yes, I'd been with a gorgeous man and had incredible sex for the first time in my life (on a clipper ship sailing through the Caribbean, no less). The energy of those memories made my body buzz with aliveness. But there was something much more profound happening to me. I felt different in my own skin—more whole and wildly freer.

In the Caribbean, I'd heard The Voice. "Drop the chip," it had said. Was it God who had spoken to me? I thought so, because who else could it have been? What might have confounded me even more is that I'd actually listened. Me, *listening*. It reminded me of the other times I'd heard a voice. The first was when I was a young girl and heard "O Gentle Presence" being sung in my dad's car the night my eye was healed. Then, of course, I'd heard that same hymn after my life had been spared in a horrible car accident. I didn't understand what I was supposed to do with this new message, *drop the chip*, but somehow, I knew to trust it. In my bones, I knew. And when I listened, a new space of grace had opened inside me. Wonderful things had ensued—falling for a gorgeous man, our romance, the sex, him giving me his worn copy of *The French Lieutenant's Woman*, scuba diving together, our meaningful conversations. I would never have considered being with a man like Sam before The Voice, and it felt like freedom. *Freedom*. It was a sensation I'd never experienced. But boy, did I feel it now. Before, I'd always considered God to be "out there," a presence that casually dropped in when I was good enough, worked hard enough, and prayed diligently enough. But for the first time, I felt certain there was a presence inside of me. It felt like a newfound power, an inner knowing. I started calling her the Golden Goddess.

I wanted to transport that whole woman, my full self and soul, back to St. Louis and into my life, but the closer I got to Missouri, the more it felt like the Golden Goddess was disintegrating. I was like a wild, tropical flower being removed from its natural habitat and planted in frozen ground. First, the flower curls over. Then the leaves begin to wilt, and finally, the stem—the flower's backbone—topples. That same thing was happening to me, and I could feel each part of me starting to wither.

Within twenty-four hours of returning to St. Louis, I was back on a plane, this time with Jim, heading to Washington, DC, for a meeting at the White House with Coddy and White House Political Director Ken Mehlman—a meeting that would determine the president's level of support for our campaign through Election Day.

Jim and I sat next to one another on the plane. He sat in the aisle seat, and I was in the middle. I looked beyond the passenger next to me and out the window.

I thought about Sam and tried to conjure up the way we had looked at one another, quietly and for hours at a time. On his pillow, on the sand, on the ship's deck, and in the sea, our faces would be inches apart, and we would stare at each other without saying anything out loud. It was the most sensual thing I had ever experienced. I did not know why Sam had looked at me like that, but I knew why I looked at him. Sam had been my mirror.

"How was your trip, Jen?" Jim asked once he'd finally arranged himself in his airplane seat and stretched his long legs.

I turned to look at him. "It was very nice and relaxing. Thank you for letting me go, Jim." I swallowed my voice as I said this, not revealing any truth. I knew he would be shocked if he found out I had hooked up with a twenty-four-year-old diving instructor, and I still did not have the proper words to adequately describe the swirl of emotions I was feeling about the direction of my life. To share even the tiniest details seemed unwise, even slightly dangerous. I had too many things to figure out first.

"Of course. It is great to see you back on track."

I let his words roll around in my mind. *Am I back on track? I feel like I'm on a different track.*

By the next afternoon, I had again returned to St. Louis and was in my office recounting for Lloyd and Miriam the outcome of our meeting at the White House. I had just finished telling them that Ken had agreed to everything Jim asked for when my Blackberry buzzed.

"Right on cue," I said, figuring Jim was emailing me. He was still in DC, holding fundraising meetings, and I knew he had a break between appointments. I halfheartedly picked up my Blackberry and scrolled to the top of my inbox to read the most recent message. That was when I saw that the email was not from Jim but from Sam—my first time hearing from him since leaving the ship three days earlier. He signed off by writing, *Don't forget to live from time to time*. I smiled.

Only a few days before, he had asked me if I'd noticed how many times I'd said "have to" in describing my life. "Why do you 'have to'?" Sam asked me. "This is your life, not a prison sentence."

I thought about his question. *Why do I have to?* I came up with many responses, all starting with "because." Because of my career. Because I've made a commitment. Because people are counting on me. Because what else am I supposed to do? None of these responses made me feel satisfied or whole.

Lloyd's loud, Southern drawl suddenly yanked me back into the present. I came to and noticed Lloyd and Miriam staring at me as I rocked back and forth in my office chair.

"Well, well, well," Lloyd said. "You look more smitten than a pig in shit."

I forced a laugh. Not because it wasn't true—it was—but because I felt invisible. No one could hear the Golden Goddess but me, and here, now, that meant I was all alone. Pain accompanied my joy; they lived side by side now and had become partners, wildly flinging one another around on the dance floor of my memories. I thought about God and wondered what she was thinking about me. My eyes had been opened and my heart had expanded, which made for uncharted living space. I did not know what the Golden Goddess wanted me to do with the new knowledge I had gleaned about myself in the past few days. *Okay, God, I dropped the chip*, I thought. *So now what?*

KANSAS CITY

Mid-June 2002 (Age 30)

A week after I returned from the Caribbean, I arrived in Kansas City to prepare for the President Bush fundraising dinner with White House Advance, the team of Secret Service members and logistics experts who arrive on-site to prepare for the president's arrival. After my car accident and before going to the Caribbean, the thought of traveling to Kansas City ahead of the team to prepare for the dinner had filled me with panic. I had been terrified of being alone—and being alone with my thoughts—for four days in a quiet hotel. Now, this trip was serving as a lifeline for me. I relished the fact that I would be gone from the campaign office for several days. I craved time on my own to think.

I bought Jeff Buckley's *Grace* album, and in my hotel room, I pressed play over and over again on my Walkman. As the title song began, the guitar harmony exploded into my ears, and I closed my eyes. The song was like a portal; memories streamed through me as I listened to it, and sometimes, I had visions of what my future could be. One night, when I could not sleep, I turned up the volume as high as it would go. I pushed down my covers and stood up in my hotel bed as the music rang through my ears, and in my tank top and underwear, I started jumping on the bed so wildly that if the hotel's management had walked into my room, they would have surmised I was either possessed or drunk, although I had not had one sip of alcohol.

On the day of the president's visit, the sun was shining as Air Force One landed at Kansas City International Airport. I had reserved one of the hotel's largest suites for Jim and Brenda to relax in before the presidential dinner, and once we got to the suite, Jim and I stretched out on the sofas while we picked at a cheese platter and debriefed on the day's events. The hotel suite was a swarm of activity, with many VIPs coming and going, but

Jim and I did what we always did. A photograph of Jim and me in that hotel suite shows each of us lying on a sofa. The couches are across from each other, and our feet dangle off the armrests. Cans of Diet Coke and the half-eaten cheese platter lie on a table between us. We look the picture of the perfect relationship between a senator-to-be and his chief of staff—the picture I had wanted to achieve for my entire career.

The Golden Goddess? I mean, *come on*. Lying on the sofa in the hotel suite across from Jim, the thought seemed ridiculous. My only thought was, *Get over yourself, Jen*.

I may not have told Jim or anyone else about what I was feeling, but, like a dam holding too much water, I could not contain the changes within me, and they began to seep out in other ways.

After the presidential dinner, when Air Force One was in the air and Jim and Brenda were on their way home to St. Louis, a group of senior congressional staff, including Miriam and me, went to a bar to go dancing. While drinking cosmopolitans and smoking a Robusto (my first-ever cigar), the Missouri congressional chiefs of staff and I danced on top of the barroom tables to Eminem's "Lose Yourself." We sang the lyrics in unison at the top of our lungs as if the song were our anthem, and we danced until the bar closed at 2:00 a.m. Throughout the night, my colleagues' shock and disbelief that I was drinking and dancing on a table was palpable. I considered that at any moment, my male colleagues might hoist me over their heads and carry me around the bar, cheering as they went. Miriam, however, looked like she was on the verge of a coronary. She kept staring at me, shock in her eyes, and saying, "I just can't believe it is you, Jen. I really can't." I could not tell whether she was horrified or happy that her legendarily uptight boss had let loose. But watching her watch me, I felt a certain kind of pride. I was having the time of my life.

DECISIONS

July 2002 (Age 30)

After my car accident, Jim's strong encouragement to take a week of R&R had landed me on a clipper ship in the Caribbean. But when I told him I was going to London for a four-day vacation to see Sam in late July, Jim had a decidedly different reaction.

"Hey, Jim, can I talk to you for a minute?" I said this one morning when he came into my office at the campaign headquarters to talk about his recent trip to Northeast Missouri.

"Sure. What's up?"

"Well, I wanted to tell you that I'm going to London for a few days in July."

"London? Why?"

"So . . . I met somebody."

"You met somebody from London?"

"Yes. When I was in the Caribbean."

"What do you mean? Who is it?"

"His name is Sam. He worked on the boat . . . I mean . . . he was one of the ship's captains."

Jim said nothing, but his horrified expression spoke volumes. His joyful countenance disappeared completely, replaced by a steeliness that I recognized. He was angry.

"No, Jen. No. This is not okay."

"What? What do you mean?"

"You don't know anything about this man, and you want to fly to Europe to see him? No. I'm sorry, Jen, but this is unacceptable. This just isn't part of the plan."

Jim's exasperated voice dripped with condescension, mirroring the tone of a father who disapproves when his teenage daughter's boyfriend keeps her out past curfew. I reacted by sitting up straighter in my office chair, the signal that I was girding myself with courage.

"I'm sorry you feel that way, Jim. But I will be going the third week in July, and I'll be gone for four days. That's the week you'll be in DC fundraising, so you won't even know I'm gone."

"Oh, I'll *know* you're gone." He paused, and then he stood up from my love seat. "Jen, don't you see how crazy this is? A woman like you . . . falling for some Crocodile Dundee?"

Crocodile Dundee? In a huff, Jim walked out of my office, slamming the door behind him. He was mad, but for the first time in my life, his disapproval would not impact my plans. I'd never directly disobeyed him before. That was an uncomfortable feeling, but not uncomfortable enough to change my mind.

ENGLAND

July 2002 (Age 30)

I had never been to England before, and my plane landed at Heathrow Airport on a Thursday morning in the middle of July. It was a sunny day and almost hot outside, even by my American standards. My heart skipped a beat when I realized my taxi was one of the iconic black English taxicabs I'd seen in the movies, and the TAXI light in the front was on full glow. I climbed inside.

"Hallo, love. Where are we going today?"

"I'm going to Knightsbridge." I gave the address.

"From California, are we?"

I started laughing. I considered myself to be the antithesis of a carefree Californian. "No, I'm actually from Washington, DC."

"Well, you would bring sunshine wherever you went, love."

I rolled my eyes and laughed. I thought, *London taxi drivers must rehearse lines like these for all the American tourists.* I opened my window as he drove into the city, and I leaned as near to the outside as I could, determined to see, smell, and hear everything I'd only watched on movie screens and imagined from the pages of books. We passed very old buildings that sat next to modern skyscrapers, shiny shops, and primeval-looking pubs; we drove by outdoor marketplaces, and we rode along the Thames. When the taxi stopped in front of Harrods of London, the driver gave me the heads-up that we were almost to my hotel. By then, I felt so full of joy I figured I could not possibly become any happier.

The taxi turned the corner, and halfway down the street, he stopped in front of a pale-yellow centuries-old hotel with white columns and the Union Jack flag flying out front. I fought every urge to scream with delight. I took a deep breath and stepped outside. It was the most romantic place I'd ever seen.

I spotted Sam on the sidewalk at the same time he spotted me. He smiled.

ENGLISH ROSES

July 2002 (Age 30)

Since high school, the Merchant Ivory production of *A Room with a View*, based on the book by E. M. Forster, has been one of my favorites. Set in Edwardian England, it tells the story of Lucy Honeychurch, a young woman who is engaged to a rigid snob of a man while being wildly in love with another, the bohemian-spirited George Emerson. Just before Lucy comes to terms with this truth about herself, her mother is gardening in their elegant garden, fighting intense gusts of wind to protect her roses. The first time I saw that movie (and I have seen it at least twenty times since), the beauty and symbolism of that scene haunted me, and I became obsessed with English roses. In fact, I loved them so much that when I bought my house on the Chesapeake Bay, I taught myself how to properly grow them and planted several varieties of David Austin English Roses outside my home. Of course, tending to those roses was the very thing that had caused me to almost lose my thumb when a thorn pricked me and caused an infection at the start of the campaign. But oh, how I still loved them.

When Sam asked me what I wanted to do during our time together, I suggested several things but only insisted on one. I wanted to find a magnificent rose garden.

We decided on Hatfield, the location of the impressive Hatfield House, the childhood home of Queen Elizabeth I, the Virgin Queen, built in the fifteenth century. One of Sam's best friends lived there, and we could stay with him. Our train left from King's Cross Station, and when we arrived, we discovered that the gates to the property had just been shut. Hatfield House was now closed for the day.

"Shit!" Sam yelled, holding the spindles of the large iron gates. "No roses!"

We walked a few blocks to his friend Tony's house. The scenic view looked like the rolling hills I had always pictured in my mind when I imagined rural England. At the back of the garden sat a large wooden dining table under a pergola covered in vines, and I knew that's where I would be spending my time for the rest of the day.

As the night moved toward morning, I became aware of Sam leaning over me to tell me it was time for bed. I put my arms around him, and he lifted me up. We went upstairs to a bed so small that we were pressed up against one another, our bare skin joined. Every muscle, every line, every rise of our bodies became exposed. With one hand around his neck and the other on the small of his back, I ached for him to find me again. And he did find me, first with his fingers and then his lips, starting at my neck and moving to my stomach. He arrived at my hip bones and covered them with his hands, his blond hair spilling across my face. A ravenousness existed between us now, brought on by the intensity of memory.

I asked myself what I saw reflected back at me when I looked into his eyes now, and whether my reflection had changed in the past seven weeks. I thought maybe it had. I felt a softness now, and a daring vulnerability. Fear was there, too, but also light, and the light radiated around everything, enveloping us. She was here, the Golden Goddess, and she was me.

When Sam fell asleep, I stared at the shape of him illuminated by the moon's soft light. I leaned over, put my hand on his chest, and watched it rise and fall with his breath as he slept.

Sleep evaded me that night. For the past few months, an inner call for stillness had been chasing me down, and it usually found me in the oddest of places. I was not naturally drawn to being still, always preferring activity to quiet, work to rest, movement over sitting. But now, stillness was tracking me, and it watched me. When it found me, it would sometimes sit right on top of my chest to keep me from moving, like a cat who was trying to get my attention.

I knew that it was God calling me, but I could not explain that to Sam.

I looked over at him. His face was serene and profoundly beautiful. I kissed him softly on his lips. Then, I got out of bed and found my clothes. Sunlight was pushing through the bedroom window, and as I was hoisting my dirty jeans over my hips, Sam stirred. He reached up and grabbed me around my waist to pull me back into bed.

"I'm going to Hatfield House to find the roses," I said.

He opened his eyes to a squint, raised one eyebrow, and looked up at me like I was insane, or still drunk.

Tony's front door was almost impossible to open, and I had to use my full force to tug on it. It squeaked so loudly when it swung open that I thought I might wake the entire neighborhood. It was Sunday morning, and the street was totally silent. I stood on the front stoop for a few moments to get my bearings, and as I began walking, I remembered the old saying about how discovering God's meaning is like chasing a wild boar in the forest. Even if you search for many days on end, you might never catch the boar; you might not even catch a glimpse of him. But there is absolutely no chance of catching the boar if you don't even attempt the chase.

The same might be said of the search for roses.

The gates to Hatfield House were open when I arrived, and I walked inside. The grounds were so silent I could hear the birds singing, and as far as I could tell, I was the only person there. The enormous red-brick manor house, built in 1485 and called the Old Palace, was so imposing that it was more ominous than attractive, and it exuded a distinct sense that the Virgin Queen herself was still inside, watching from the upstairs windows. I walked past the house, and when I turned the corner just beyond it, I saw the massive gardens—roses and boxwoods and hydrangeas and lavender as far as I could see. I walked over to the roses. Different rose varieties in pinks and whites were planted next to dozens of other flowers. To be all alone among so much loveliness made me feel like I was trespassing. I looked around before I sat down on the ground, and I was very still.

It was early, just after 9:00 a.m., and I could already tell it was going to be another hot day. Sweat, shiny and sticky, poured from my face, and I felt gross wearing my clothes for a second day in a row. As I sat on the grass, swarms of insects buzzed by my face, and I shooed them away with my hand. A rabbit hopped behind the moppy hydrangeas, blue and white and as big as teacups. Bees buzzed around the flowers. I was leaning back and looking at the white clouds floating above me when I was suddenly transported to lying on the carpeted floor in my apartment after my car accident. Panic descended on me. How many hours had I spent there?

Then, I thought about the stillness.

What did I need to do to change my life? Of course, like all questions of this nature, I could only find the answer by looking inside myself. I was the only one stopping me from listening to my own heart and freeing myself to make a decision. I had no ties to anything—no husband, no house, and, come November, not even a job. After the campaign ended, I would have no responsibility to any other person, and there was nothing preventing me from packing up and starting a new life. *Listen to your heart and follow it* was the thought that came. If I didn't try, the only person I would disappoint would be myself.

I sat there for almost an hour before I stood to walk back to Tony's house.

BRIGHTON

July 2002 (Age 30)

On my last day in England, we took the train to Brighton, a seaside town on the English Channel. Just off the pebble beach, we stopped at a tiny market with a striped awning and colorful vegetables in wooden boxes to buy olives, bread, and cheese for lunch. We spread ourselves out on the lawn at a park near the sea and ate, listening to a man play guitar and sing Beatles songs. For the first time in four days, very few words passed between us, not because there was nothing to say but because there was too much.

In the late afternoon, we went to a pub where we ordered Guinness and sat outside in the sun. Finally, being the braver of us right then, Sam voiced the subject that was on both of our minds. "How are you feeling about going home tomorrow, Jen?"

I put my head in my hands, feeling I had permission to let my dread overtake me now that the subject had been broached. I fought like hell not to fall apart. "Sam, I am a thirty-year-old woman with the most impressive résumé of anyone I know, and I have no idea what I want to do with the rest of my life. But one thing I do know—I cannot continue to work in politics." This was the first time I'd said this out loud, and it felt good to hear these words coming from my own lips. Terrifying, but good. Saying it aloud strengthened me.

He leaned over to me, put his hand gently on my leg, and held it there. "Why don't you consider living abroad for a while?"

Living abroad had been on my mind, at least fleetingly. I'd thought about trying my hand at teaching somewhere overseas. But as each new idea came to me, I just as quickly threw it out the window. I tried to explain this to Sam.

"I've been thinking about Italy, and also France. My law school mentor said once that he might be able to get me a job teaching in France, where he went to school. But I don't speak any other languages besides English. I haven't spoken French since high school."

"Well, what about Australia?"

Australia? I thought, then repeated the word out loud. "Australia?" I sat up higher in my chair. For whatever reason, living in Australia had never dawned on me.

"Australia is one of the best places I've ever lived," Sam continued. The laid-back people, the beautiful landscape, the cosmopolitan cities, the wildlife, the oceans . . ."

I only partially heard him. I felt like all the signposts were finally pointing in the same direction. A light turned on inside my head.

Why not think about moving to Australia? I thought. *What do I have to lose?*

CHAPTER 8

Chasing the Boar, Part I

POEMS

1978 (Age 7)

Here is how my mom recounts my nightly bedtime routine from the age of five onward:

Every night, about twenty minutes before my official bedtime, I would walk into the kitchen and grab the largest glass I could find. My dad had six huge green drinking glasses that were twice the size of normal drinking glasses, and as a teenager, I would stand on my tippy-toes to reach the cabinet's top shelf and retrieve one. But when I was young, I would need to scramble up on top of the counter to reach them. I did this every night.

With my glass in hand, I would open the refrigerator. I would not use the glass for water or juice or even soda. Instead, I stuffed as many fruits and vegetables into it as I possibly could. Iceberg lettuce, carrots, celery, and apples of all varieties—the bright green Granny Smiths being my perennial favorite. "A little rabbit," my mom called me.

Once the glass was stuffed to its brim, I carried it to my bedroom and turned out the light. My flashlight would stay hidden under my pillow, and as soon as everything was organized *just so*, I would switch the flashlight on. For hours, far past the time my parents gave me for official lights-out, I would munch on my cup's treasures while reading and reenacting my favorite stories. *Little House on the Prairie*, *Anne of Green Gables*, *A Little Princess*, and, always, poems by Shel Silverstein. I owned every one of his poetry books and had committed many of his *Where the Sidewalk Ends* verses to memory. Surrounded by the eerie shadows dancing on my wall, I would recite the poems in a loud whisper using funny voices that depended on both my mood and the poem—the silly man who forgot his pants, Hector the Collector, Ridiculous Rose who ate with her toes, and Terrible Teresa who asked for a pancake from the middle of the tall stack. Sometimes, I would angle the flashlight to watch my own shadow dramatically gesticulating on the walls of my room. My imagination was so intensely wild that it felt like a small death to shut it down for the night. In those late hours, my bedroom became both my stage and my sanctuary.

At our house on Maple Street in Hinsdale, a.k.a. the World Dryer House, my bedroom had a pitched ceiling that made my shadow act a true sight to behold, almost like it was taking place in a diorama. One spring night when I was about seven, my windows were open, and it was very late—hours after I was supposed to be asleep. I sat cross-legged at the end of my bed with my flashlight lying behind me to perfectly project my image onto the wall and the slanted ceiling. In front of me was an imaginary steering wheel attached to my imaginary championship race car, which I was gripping so tightly and turning so sharply to win my make-believe race that I did not see my dad enter my bedroom door.

"WHAT ARE YOU DOING?" He yelled so loudly the room shook, and as I turned to face him, he put his hands on my shoulders.

Then my memory goes black, locked somewhere in the recesses of my brain. For years, I've tried to revive it, but without luck.

On my first visit to therapist Nichoel Kimmerle, MA, LMFT, in January 2022, I asked about this half memory and whether she could help me recapture it. She responded firmly that some memories are meant to be left alone.

"I don't know if this is one of those," she went on. "But if it is, it may be that your mind is protecting you from what is unhealthy for you to revisit."

I nodded at this answer, understanding her meaning.

AGNOSTIC

2003–2013 (Ages 32–42)

I recently heard the poet Christian Wiman say on a podcast that he believes God calls some people to a place of unbelief in order for their faith to take on new forms inside them.

"I am convinced," he said, "that the same God that might call me to sing of God at one time might call me at another to sing of godlessness." I nodded so vigorously that my neck looked like it was on a spring. I have lived this exact truth. For many years, I refused to pray. The inclination was always present inside me, and it tried persistently to make itself known. But each time, I chased it down and put a stop to it.

"I do not want to believe in you anymore," I said to God. "Please go away."

It was not lost on me that I was speaking to a God I didn't want to believe in.

Chasing the Boar, Part I

I stopped believing in God when I moved to Australia, only five months after I'd discovered the Golden Goddess in the Caribbean. The truth was that when my plane landed in Melbourne, exhilaration and excitement pulsed through my body—along with deep and profound anger. In the past year and a half, my life—my entire life, which I had worked so hard to painstakingly build—had been ripped away from me. And the worst thing about it was that *I* was the one who did the ripping.

I felt that God had let me down. I'd been faithful every day of my life, and God had only punished me for it. I'd prayed and prayed and almost lost my thumb. I'd had a car accident that almost killed me. I'd been sued and slandered in the news. My husband had been a cheater, and though I hadn't loved him, I had been loyal to him, which made me feel the sting of wasted years. I felt like such a fool. What's more, the career I had given my life to had turned out to be hollow, maybe worse. While I burned with possibility in Australia, I also seethed with rage.

I wouldn't know until years later that pain—going through it, leaning in to it rather than running away—brings the transformation we long for. Feeling the very edges of pain's rawness, and the way it wraps around our hearts and bones, is what springboards us into a new place. In the decades since, I've seen it played out time and again, that cycle of pain transforming me into something larger, freer, and more whole as a woman. But pain feels horrible, hurting us on a soul level, and transformation can take a very long time. Somehow, though, we have to keep listening, keep being still, keep holding on to the knowing inside of us—that beautiful Golden Goddess who tells us things. But I didn't know it then. And so, I ran from the pain—and my life. I ran as far as I could go.

In Australia, I stopped tying the Golden Goddess to God and decided instead that she belonged exclusively to me. I wanted to believe that *I* was the foundation for her greatness and mystery;

I was the one solely responsible for making any good happen in my life. Australia was a time to focus on discovering myself, and it was there that I abandoned my search for God.

It was time, I reasoned, to take matters into my own hands.

But God kept peeking under the covers of my life and wouldn't leave me alone. I felt this in small and large ways, and it really pissed me off. The more I ignored her, or him, or whatever God is (or isn't), the more annoying she became, until I'd feel the sensation of God land in the worst, most visible place in my mind's eye. "*A-hem*?" she would whisper, looking at me like a fly sitting on my nose. "I'm right here!"

Finally, I asked God if we could just take a hiatus, and that seemed to work better than anything else at giving me a bit of room to breathe.

Without God in my life, discovering who I was as a person and a woman, and figuring out what I was supposed to do next in my life, became the abstract things I gave my life to. Discovery, that is, and writing the first draft of my memoir. In the span of three years, I traveled to five countries on three continents. At bars and coffee shops; on beaches around the world; under trees and bridges; on planes, trams, and buses; in hotel swimming pools; and in the middle of deserts with camels baying in the distance, I wrote. In time, I had written over 150,000 words on 275 single-spaced pages for my memoir. It was a monumental effort, but even though I didn't know it then, writing proved to be the easy part. Editing, both on the page and in life, would be so much harder.

MONASTERY, CAMBRIDGE, MASSACHUSETTS

October 2012 (Age 41)

A monk, a priest, three men, and three women sat in a circle inside a small room. I am not setting up the punch line to a joke;

this scene really happened. Eight people, including me, looked at one another inside a silent monastery in Cambridge, Massachusetts, and the monk spoke first.

"We are honored to have you here at the Society of Saint John the Evangelist. I will be leading your guided retreat, and I look forward to our journey together."

I hadn't attended a church service for over ten years, and laying eyes on a real monk was a first for me. Everyone else in the circle was religious, and I felt deeply unsettled. The curiosity I'd had about visiting a 150-year-old monastery began morphing into serious regret. For starters, the sparseness of my tiny bedroom freaked me out. With enough space for only a tiny cot, a small desk, and a Bible, I now understood why they'd called it a "cell" at check-in. What was I supposed to do for four days? Then, there was the silence. The Society of Saint John the Evangelist, or SSJE, prided itself on its history as a *silent* monastery. Speaking was forbidden—except in group retreat sessions like the one I was attending.

While the monk and my circle mates talked, I looked out of the large picture window. Just across the Charles River, I could see Harvard University's campus, lined with the gold and orange colors of fall in New England. Clouds floated in the sky. I was lost in the scene until I noticed Gary staring at me. When our eyes locked, he smiled.

I'd been regularly meeting with Gary, or more appropriately, Reverend and Rector of St. Stephen's Episcopal Church Gary Jones, for the past month. At our first meeting, he hadn't flinched when I'd shared my struggles, or even when I told him I wasn't sure I believed in God anymore. This earned him instant credibility. He'd also listened to me without any attempt to push me in a certain religious direction—also a first.

"Finding a way to honor the restlessness inside you is the ongoing struggle of every deep thinker" was one of the first things

Gary said to me. For the first time in years, I felt seen. That was how I felt in my conversations with him, and that's why I'd considered his suggestion to visit SSJE. I would have laughed if anyone else had suggested the idea. In fact, I think I laughed when Gary first mentioned it.

"I'm not sure this God stuff is for me, Gary. I'm the least likely candidate for a monastery, of all places."

"SSJE is not about religious piety. It is about being still and finding enough quiet to hear your own voice."

So, by October, I'd signed up for a four-day retreat. I decided it was time to find an antidote for the burning disquiet smoldering inside my body. I admired Gary, and I wanted to discover the same sense of peace he displayed in my own life.

The monk leading our retreat was named Brother David. He wore a long black robe and a clerical collar like the one I'd sometimes seen Gary wear. His pleasant expression was tempered by a seriousness that kept me on my guard. I felt nervous about coming across as stupid in front of this room full of lifelong Anglicans.

Brother David was reading a passage from the Book of John about a man who had been blind since birth:

> *The disciples asked Jesus, "Who sinned, this man or his parents that he was born blind?"*
>
> *"Neither," Jesus replied. "This happened so that the works of God may be displayed in him."*

Brother David paused before asking us a question. "How do you feel about what Jesus said?" Someone in the group mentioned that God never leaves us, and another said that parents aren't perfect, so it was fortunate that children didn't pay for their parents' sins. I considered these comments feeble, and without thinking, I blurted, "But what is God's responsibility?"

All eyes, including Gary's, turned to me. Brother David asked, "What do you mean?"

"Are you saying that God will just leave the blind man blind without any hope? What kind of God is that?"

Gary eyed me carefully. He was used to my pointed directness but clearly didn't know how Brother David would react.

"I cannot speak to what God might do for the man's sight," Brother David said. "But I do know that God will never leave us without hope. To me, *that* is the point of this story."

I found his answer profoundly unsatisfying and even a little condescending. Who wanted a God that stood by and did nothing while we humans *hoped* for help? I didn't speak again that day. After dinner, I went to my room, a.k.a. my cell, to lie down on my cot. I closed my eyes and said out loud, "Okay, God. Here we go again. I'm trying here. Are you going to leave me high and dry? Again?"

I contemplated the Bible story of the blind man again and recalled my good friend Harry. My erstwhile boss and closest friend from my Capitol Hill days, Harry, who was twenty years my senior, had also worked for Jim Talent in the House. No one could make me laugh like Harry did. He smoked so many cigars that his smell traveled ahead of him, and his red wine and vodka drinking were legendary. He lived to play golf and tell hilarious stories about all the members of Congress he knew. We worked together closely and traveled on business trips often.

One afternoon, when we were returning to DC from Phoenix on a Southwest Airlines flight, I waited for over twenty minutes while Harry emptied his pockets at airport security, removing metal cigar cutters, gold lighters, multicolored golf tees, and two wads of keys. He sounded like a one-man band as he attempted to walk through the magnetometer three times, his pockets jingling. Each time, the security officers turned him back for more unloading—a pocketknife, a few silver dollars, a screwdriver for his sunglasses. Finally, we made it to our gate. He was so exasperated by then that he put on his dark sunglasses and suggested that I lie to the airline workers, telling them he was blind and required early boarding. When I outwardly bristled at his suggestion, he handed me two twenty-dollar bills and told me to go buy him a cane at the airport bookstore.

"You're a lunatic," I clapped back. "Go buy yourself your own damn cane."

"I can't," Harry said. "I'm blind."

An hour later, midflight, with his two empty airplane bottles of Grey Goose sitting on his tray table, Harry smacked his lips.

"Jen," he exclaimed with his trademark cheeky smile. "You always make even the shittiest things a hell of a lot more fun."

Lying on my cot in my monastery cell, I experienced a moment of connection when I remembered this. Could it be that like the best of friends, God sustains us even when we are in life's most horrible places, like navigating airport security, or being trapped in a burning car? Maybe one of the reasons for trusting God is to redeem what is wrong with the world by having the courage to witness it.

RESURRECTION

October 2012 (Age 41)

The next morning, I started noticing a pattern. On the walls around the monastery, and even inside my cell, there were dozens of icons and pictures of the crucified Jesus with his overlapping feet nailed painfully to the cross and his face wearing an expression of anguish. In Christian Science, we always focused on the *resurrected* Jesus—never the crucified one—and I found the crucified version maudlin and not very hopeful (or helpful, for that matter). I decided to ask Brother David about it during our next group session.

"Why do you focus on the depressing image of Jesus being crucified? I mean, it's *everywhere.*"

Brother David and every other person in the room looked at me aghast, cementing my reputation as the heathen I surely was. Under pressure from their horrified glances, I attempted to clarify what I meant.

"What I'm trying to ask is, why not surround yourselves with more joyful images of Jesus's resurrection?"

The clarification helped, and I could see in Brother David's face that he was making the link. I'd gotten him thinking.

"Well, in order to have the resurrection, Jesus had to endure the pain of the crucifixion."

"Sure, okay. But why *dwell* on the pain rather than the hopeful result?"

"Because most of life is much more like the crucifixion," he said. "Jesus on the cross reflects that."

I looked up at the spot on the wall where a ten-inch Jesus, skinny and bleeding, was nailed to a wooden cross, and it infuriated me. I was already confused and depressed. Why in God's name would I want to be reminded of it? When the session was over, I walked outside and pulled a menthol cigarette from my pocket. I'd smoked on and off since being in Australia and usually kept a pack of cigarettes hidden in a drawer or my suitcase when I traveled. Once I had walked far down the sidewalk and away from the monastery, I lit it and took a long drag. I breathed out, and the gray smoke swirled around my head.

No, I thought. *No way. I don't need constant reminders of how hard life is. These people are nuts.*

CHAPTER 9

Chasing the Boar, Part II

SANCTUARY, LAST DAY AT SSJE

October 2012 (Age 41)

My last morning at the monastery was a Sunday, the day of SSJE's formal church service. I sat near the back of the sanctuary, off to one side, so I wouldn't draw attention to the fact that I had no idea what I was doing. Even though I'd been meeting with Gary for a while, I had never been to an Episcopal church service before—and I hadn't been to any church service in over a decade. One of the monks read the Bible from the pulpit, incense burned, and the brothers chanted Psalms. My confusion reached new heights, but it was also quite beautiful to watch.

About midway through the service, I felt a pang of pain in my ribs. Since my car accident, these pangs still happened often. They could sometimes be debilitating, and I would need to lie down. Today, the pain seemed manageable. I put my hand on my ribs to massage them, which helped. Then, suddenly, in one of the rows of people near the front, I swore I saw my dad. My disbelief met my curiosity, although I knew my eyes must be playing tricks on me. I bobbed and weaved my head and neck to get a better view, but I couldn't find him again. I closed my eyes and took a long, slow breath, and as I did, my mind drifted back to a long-forgotten memory. Every morning of my childhood, I would walk downstairs to the family room and come upon my dad sitting in his favorite navy blue leather chair with his eyes closed. His hands sat peacefully on the Bible in his lap, and he looked like a weatherworn angel who had seen a lot of life but remained determined to serve God. As I stood watching him inside my memory, he opened his eyes and smiled at me, startling me. I breathed in sharply and opened my eyes.

The memory of my dad was so real that I started to cry. I felt swept under by anger and sadness. I cried so hard that the sweet, gray-haired older woman in the seat next to me handed me a small package of tissues from her handbag. She patted my arm lovingly, and I took hold of her hand. We sat there for several minutes, two complete strangers holding hands in church. When it came time for the brothers to move into spots around the sanctuary to take confession, I walked over to Brother David.

I knelt next to him on the black-and-white tile floor. I was crying so hard he could not understand my words, but he put his hand softly on the crown of my head.

"What is it, my child?" He leaned in to hear me through my sobs.

"I don't know what God wants from me." I wept through gritted teeth.

It was clear he could not hear my garbled words, but his hand still rested on my head. "God loves you so much. That, my child, is what you can know for sure."

When I left the monastery later that afternoon, I could not identify anything I'd learned, but I felt different, altered slightly into a more beautiful and truer version of myself. But like all divine things, this moment of understanding was fleeting.

What lasted was the new space that opened inside of me. A place of mystery and quiet, it would sustain me when nothing else could.

CHAPTER 10

Healing

TRANSFORMING PAIN

August 2, 2012 (Age 40)

In a letter to *Time* magazine, two-time Newbery Medal–winning children's author Kate DiCamillo posed this question about writing difficult truths in books: *How do we tell the truth and make that truth bearable?* Then, she posited her best guess at an answer: *Love*, she wrote. *By loving the world and telling the truth about it at the very same time.*

Nine years after returning from Australia, and three months after my drunk interview with Senator Allen in downtown Richmond, I sat at the edge of my parents' bed watching my dad struggle to breathe. My sixty-nine-year-old father was under the covers, unable to move. Once a tall, athletic, handsome man with broad shoulders and a gait like a cheetah's, he'd lost sixty pounds from not eating. His gaunt body looked like a skeleton with skin stretched across the bones. Large, bulbous growths stuck out of his head and neck, and his legs, always lean and muscular, had swollen to twice their normal size. His body emitted an almost intolerable stench.

When my dad died, it was August, and I was sitting on a beach in Duck, North Carolina, while my two little boys splashed in the Atlantic Ocean. I answered my cell phone, and the poor reception garbled my mom's voice. I started walking back to the beach house we'd rented for the week.

"Jen? Jen, can you hear me?"

"Yes, Mom. I can hear you."

"Your dad died this morning, honey."

I sat down on the pavement where I was standing, which happened to be in the middle of a residential street.

"Oh," I said. "Are you okay, Mom?"

"Yes. I'll be fine." She said this in the way she always did, whether she was on the verge of a sneeze or a mental breakdown.

"What happens next?"

"They're going to take him away soon."

"Right."

She kept talking, but I didn't hear her.

Franciscan priest Richard Rohr, an author and teacher who would become a lifeline for me a few years later, wrote that if we do not transform our pain, we will most assuredly transmit it—usually to our family, and especially our children. What I felt in that moment was a deep and raw transmittal of fury. My entire body seized up under the weight of it. My awareness of the rage did not sit on the surface of my body but instead felt visceral, and it came on so suddenly I did not know its origin. I actually considered whether, in passing, my father could have somehow figured out a way to teleport the pain from his body into mine, at the beach 170 miles away. Or maybe I'd finally given myself permission to feel things I'd mostly blocked during his lifetime. Both small and huge memories descended on me. My dad informing me casually, over dinner one night during my college years, that I could no longer train to be a singer (after more than a decade of intense effort) because music wasn't a "real" college major. Not trusting me, as a woman, to be alone with men. Not allowing me to go on a college art history trip to Italy while at the same time financially supporting my brother on a monthlong excursion through Europe and a semester in Ireland. Catching him watching porn in his late sixties after a lifetime of holding me to impossible religious and moral standards based on the premise that women should not enjoy sex or have sex outside of marriage. The relentless, unforgiving work ethic he imposed on me, and his exacting views about the importance of climbing the mountain to reach God—beliefs that caused me to ignore my inner truths until I nearly died.

When I looked up, I realized I was still sitting in the middle of the street.

"I love you, Mom, but I'm not going to come home now."

"You're not?"

"No. I need to be here with my family. But call me anytime." It felt oddly empowering to draw this line in the sand, and I felt not even a twinge of guilt as I hung up the phone.

I stood and dusted off the back of my legs to free the small specks of gravel sticking to my skin. I walked inside our rental house and out onto the balcony. I watched the waves of the Atlantic Ocean as the seagulls squawked above. I don't know how long I sat out there, but I did not cry.

MANDORLAS AND BONFIRES, EMERY HOUSE, WEST NEWBURY, MASSACHUSETTS

January 2014 (Age 42)

Fifteen months after my first visit, and a year and a half after my dad died, I went back to SSJE, this time to the monastery's sister property in a rural town called West Newbury, about fifty miles outside of Boston. Emery House was a typical historic New England house with wide wood siding painted bright yellow. It sat in the middle of a working farm with grassy fields leading downhill to a lake surrounded by tall, leafy trees.

I'd requested a private meeting with Brother Curtis, a monk whom I had not yet met. I'd been receiving SSJE's daily email meditations for over a year, and Brother Curtis's sermons had deeply inspired me. One in particular was so moving that I kept a copy folded inside my briefcase. Called "Wrestling with God," this sermon suggests that the only way out of the dungeon of secrets from our past is to open the prison doors and let in the light. "It's not this piece of your history that is walled off," he wrote about painful memories. "It's you who is walled in, not free, not fully alive." These words spoke to me on the deepest of levels.

On my second morning there, Brother Curtis was waiting for me in a small room on the lower level of the house. Wearing a long robe and clerical collar, what first struck me about him was the wisdom in his eyes. He looked like a person who knew what he was talking about. I shook his hand and thanked him for meeting with me. He invited me to sit in one of two chairs beside the windows that overlooked the wide meadow around Emery House. A small candle burned on the table between us.

I only had one hour with him, so I began to quickly list my troubles: Feeling burdened by my past. Confusion about who I was. Confusion about God. Shame. Sadness. The constant, gnawing need to write about how I was feeling but having the complete inability to do so. *Loss. Loss. Loss.* As I spoke, I had a hard time returning Brother Curtis's gaze. I looked down, picking at the fabric on my black jeans. When I stopped talking, there was a long silence between us before I looked up again. "As you can tell," I said, "I'm having a really hard time, Brother Curtis."

He did not say anything, but he did not look away, either. He let a few long moments of silence pass before opening the top drawer of the table next to him. He pulled out a small pad of notepaper and a pen. In the center of the paper, he drew two circles that slightly overlapped. As he tapped the left circle with the tip of his pen, he looked over at me. "What would you say are your best qualities, Jen?"

I thought for a moment. "Discipline. Hard work. Loyalty."

"Ah, yes. Great," Father Curtis said. "I can see those being absolutely true for you. They have probably been true about you since you were a little girl." He continued, "What about where you feel weakest?"

"Well, contrary to my behavior today, I have a hard time being vulnerable. I also don't like leaving anything to chance."

"Thank you for sharing that with me, Jen."

I watched his pen trace the lines that made up the overlapping part of the two circles. It was the shape of an oval.

"This part in between the overlapping circles—it's called the mandorla. *Mandorla* meaning *almond*, in Italian. Ancient Christians believed that the mandorla was the eye to our souls, the gateway to our spiritual selves. See, the almond is even shaped like an eye."

I nodded at him, acknowledging that I saw it.

"The mandorla is a place of mystery, the place where the beautiful and the shadowy parts of us converge. This convergence is what gives us spiritual strength. It reflects what the Apostle Paul says about our strength being made perfect in weakness."

I'd never thought about this that way before. To me, strength was always good and weakness was always bad.

Brother Curtis continued, "Ancient Christians knew that gold was purified by fire—and, in the same way, our souls are transformed when our strengths and our weaknesses clash inside of us. Our souls are refined by that struggle—like gold in fire. This is what is represented in the image of the mandorla—the eye—which is the ultimate seer of our lives."

He handed me the piece of paper.

"While you're here, think about how you can learn to embrace your weaknesses. You can stop running from them now," Brother Curtis said. "They are meant to purify you when you quietly face them. But purification takes time and an enormous amount of heat, which can be very uncomfortable. You don't need to feel scared anymore, Jen. God is right here with you."

ASHES

April 2014 (Age 43)

I saw Brother Curtis one more time, this time in Richmond at the church I now regularly attended, St. Stephen's Episcopal, where Gary was the rector. And, at long last, I finally began to pray again.

Every night, I would take out my flashlight and read, just like I had when I was a child. I read the Book of Ezekiel in the Bible. For as often as I'd read the Bible when I was growing up, I never knew about the prophet Ezekiel, and I'm not sure why. In the story, Ezekiel has a vision of God leading him through a valley with thousands of bones lying on the ground. He walks back and forth through the valley, wading through bones so dry and brittle that all hope for life is gone. It's a very creepy scene, and while Ezekiel walks, God says to him, "Son of man, can these bones live?" That, to me, was The Question. Can dead bones and dead souls have a second chance at life?

I kept reading as God commanded Ezekiel to speak to the dead bones. As he does so, at the exact same time, God breathes.

I just love this, the image of God breathing—like a person drawing in a big breath before blowing up a balloon or when emerging from the water in a pool. God's breath enters the dry bones, and they suddenly rise up and are made alive. In the quiet of my dark bedroom, I would then listen for the sound of my own breath. In. Out. In. Out. That's when it occurred to me that maybe my own breath was also the breath of God.

When I met with Brother Curtis at St. Stephen's in mid-April, he had me write down every one of my sadnesses and regrets on a piece of paper. This took quite a while, and when I was done, I folded my paper in half.

"Now," he said. "It's time to let it burn."

We walked to a small fire pit on the church grounds. He turned to give me privacy while I pitched the paper into the flames. The paper curled at the edges before it incinerated, and I watched the smoky ashes fly high into the sky.

BODY WORK

November 2021 (Age 50)

I'd been seeing John, the barefoot bohemian massage therapist, for a little over a year when he told me it was time to start seeing a psychotherapist. There were a lot of reasons for this. For starters, I kept bursting into tears every time he touched me in certain places—my ribs, for example, or my lower abdomen. He also mentioned that I seemed to have teensy-weensy control issues that came into play when he attempted to work on me, especially my legs. A stiffness akin to rigor mortis would set in when he touched them, making it nearly impossible for him to manipulate my muscles.

"You have some kind of trauma or deep fear embedded inside your lower limbs," he said. "I've rarely seen anything like it before. Maybe only two or three times in all my decades of work."

So yes, okay, I still had a few unresolved issues. I knew this—I mean, *duh*. But I was terrified to go to a therapist. She might learn about The Monster, and then what would I do?

"Why are you resisting seeing someone?" he asked me pointedly. It was a fair question.

"Maybe because it will be confirmation that I'm as messed up as I think I am." I laughed at my own joke, my attempt to make light of the situation.

He didn't laugh. "We're all messed up, Jen. The question is whether you want to do something about it."

John was nothing if not brutally honest. He wrote a name down on a tiny piece of paper, folded it, and handed it to me. I opened it: *Nichoel Kimmerle*.

I looked up at him.

"I doubt she's taking on any new clients," John said. "But let's see if we can't get you in. She is the best there is."

CHAPTER 11

Last Two Months of the Campaign: September and October 2002

INVICTUS

September 2002 (Age 31)

When we are broken and begin to heal, we do not stand still, ruminating on the pain that we are leaving behind. We run toward what is healing us. We run to the place where we feel the beams of hope beginning to shine on us again. After all, hope is the common denominator in reminding us that we are alive.

During the campaign's final months, I sat outside on the deck of my apartment at night, my back propped against the wall and my legs stretched out in front of me. I had no patio furniture, and my only view was of the parking lot. But even though it was sticky with humidity, the outdoor air filled my lungs with freshness. I would balance my laptop on my legs and research Australian universities with the hope of finding a fellowship so I could try my hand at teaching. Mosquitoes buzzed in my ears and insects crashed into my computer screen, drawn by the light. Every night, I sat there for hours. Within a week, I had narrowed my options down to the universities that were in cities where I wanted to live: the University of Melbourne and the University of Sydney.

As the days progressed, a new Jen started to emerge. She felt big and so bold that she could be a little scary. She was, of course, me—but not the same me as I'd known before. I'd always been supremely confident about my professional talents, and I imbued a confidence that was unique for a woman of my age, but what I'm talking about here was a different thing entirely. Like one of those Russian nesting dolls, there was another skin inside of me holding another Jen, and she was just below the surface. She started expanding into every nook of my body and mind. She was kind, but you did not want to mess with her—if you did, she'd take you out back and kick your ass. Inside, the new Jen felt like a mixed martial artist with gnarly tattoos and a shaved head. I didn't look like her on the outside; on the outside, my appearance was just the same. But inside, I was becoming a badass rebel.

I was not owned anymore. No thing or person had any rights to me—not a job, a boss, a mortgage, a husband, a parent, or a religion. For the first time in my life, I was the master of my fate and the captain of my soul, just like in William Ernest Henley's poem "Invictus." I was beginning to understand the edges of that kind of power now. The power came from within, and from a place so deep in my soul that no other person could touch it.

But you can't have a badass MMA fighter rebel show up without destabilizing those around you, including the people you love. Ultimately, this new Jen would exact her price, and because I was her and she was me, she would survive, even be strengthened by the experience. But that didn't mean I and those around me would escape without paying a price. We did.

BOSSES

September 2002 (Age 31)

On a morning in late September, Jim walked into my office and sat down on my sofa. I threw him a can of Diet Coke, and as we talked for the next forty-five minutes about the run-up to the end of the campaign, I thought, *This is the time to tell him, Jen.* I braced myself for the right opening in the conversation. When he stood up to go, I panicked.

"Uh, Jim," I anxiously croaked. "I'm sorry. I need to talk with you about something personal. Would you mind staying a few more minutes?"

He looked at me nervously and sat down again. As he stared across the room at me, my mind went totally and completely blank. I couldn't think. My brain and mouth felt like they were filled with fluff, like I had cotton balls stuck to my tongue and the cavity around my brain.

"Jim."

"Yes, Jen."

"You have been the best boss I have ever had, and you know how much I care for you and Brenda."

He nodded. "We feel the same way about you."

"But you know I've been really unhappy for a long time. I know you know this. Since my car accident. Something has been 'off.'"

He was staring at me, and I willed myself to continue.

"It's politics, Jim. I don't think I'm supposed to be working in politics anymore."

He scrunched up his face and scoffed. "What are you talking about?"

"Let me be clear. I will continue to pour my heart and soul into this campaign. I will do everything I can to make sure you win. I give you my word on that, my bond, and I swear it to you. But when the campaign is over, I need to leave."

He looked at me like I'd asked him to take a hit of heroin on live TV. His mouth fell open, and he was silent for several seconds. He spoke first.

"You think I'm going to lose," he said, sounding equal parts defeated and accusatory.

"Good God, no. Jim, no. That's not it." I jumped up, horrified that this was how my words had come across. "That's not it at all!"

"You think I'm going to lose, so you're cutting out now. That's it, isn't it? You're going to work with Coddy at the White House, aren't you? I knew it."

I felt sick. This was not at all what I had planned. I could see the despair in his eyes, and I thought I might throw up.

"Jim, no. No, no, no. I'm not going to the White House. I'm not going to work for anyone else. I'm leaving politics. There is no one I'd rather work for than you."

He looked at me dubiously.

"I'm moving to Australia, Jim."

"*Australia*?" He shouted the word like it was the wrong answer on a TV game show.

"Yes. I've gotten a fellowship at the University of Melbourne Law School. They hired me very quickly."

"*You already have a job and you're just now telling me?!*" He was apoplectic now, his voice at a fever pitch.

"I needed to make sure, Jim," I said, realizing how desperate I sounded. I took a breath to recalibrate and sat back down. "I have to try something new. I'm yours through the end of the campaign. I am here for you twenty-four seven. But I am moving to Australia. Please try to understand. This has nothing to do with you and everything to do with me. Please understand, Jim, please."

I felt like I was breaking up with a boyfriend. I put my fingers on my chin as a sign to myself that it was time to shut my mouth.

It took a long time before Jim said something. I did not look at him. I was looking at my lap, embarrassed, scared, and totally unsure of myself. When he began to speak, he started slowly and quietly before he raised his voice, both in tone and volume, to a level I had not heard before. He. Was. Pissed.

"This is not what I was thinking at all, Jen. What I need is to have you in Washington as my chief of staff and Lloyd for me here." After he said this, he really started to roll and began speaking to me as if I were five-year-old Chrissy.

"Have you talked to anyone about this? Have you really thought about what you are giving up? What job will you have? You'll never get another job in politics again if you do this. You know that, right?"

His rapid-fire questions came at me fast. I felt like I was being scolded. I took a deep breath, and my confidence rose. This was what I'd learned to do as a little girl when my dad would grill me. I looked directly at Jim, and I answered his questions one by one without any emotion. No, I didn't know how long I'd be in Australia. No, I wouldn't consider postponing my move. No, I couldn't commit to rejoining his Senate team in six months.

The more questions I answered, the more authoritative I became. Slowly, I came back to my center, and I peppered the rest of our conversation with things I'd left out, including some details about teaching and writing. I also reminded myself to have patience. Trying something new had been on my mind since my car accident almost five months before, but Jim was hearing my thoughts for the first time. I had to give him space to process without getting angry at his immediate reaction, which I had always suspected would be equal parts shock and fury. He got up to leave my office. With one hand on my doorknob, he turned to look at me.

"You know, what concerns me as much as anything is the thought of you out there falling in love with some Crocodile Dundee." Then he walked out of my office.

Jesus. We're back on the Crocodile Dundee thing, again? I knew it was meant to be a swipe at Sam—more specifically, it was a swipe at the perceived bad decision-making that led me to be with someone like Sam. This infuriated me, just as Jim knew it would. I hadn't even mentioned Sam as he played no part in my upcoming Australia plans. But I let it go. There was nothing more to say.

THE PROVING GROUND

September 2002 (Age 31)

I read G. Bruce Knecht's book *The Proving Ground* in one day. Sam had recommended it to me when I was in England.

Since the inaugural race in 1945, hundreds of maxi yachts have converged in Sydney Harbour every Boxing Day to race against one another, going six hundred miles south to Hobart in Tasmania. Grueling and dangerous, it is considered to be one of the world's top-three offshore sailing races.

The Proving Ground tells the story of the 1998 race, when a cyclone hit the Tasman Sea in the middle of the event. The waves became unnavigable, and there were eighty-mile-an-hour wind gusts. The Australian navy had to send twenty-five ships and thirty-five airplanes directly into the cyclone to save the sailors. Sixty boats sank, and many people died.

I had never been on a maxi yacht, but I'd been on a boat in a storm. The book reminded me of skippering the little white Sunfish in Glen Lake when I was fourteen. However, racing a maxi yacht through a cyclone on the Tasman Sea was a whole different story.

The Proving Ground was a story about taking risks. I knew I was going to love Australia.

KARMA

October 2002 (Age 31)

I woke in the darkness to what felt like a thump, and I opened my eyes. I saw the familiar contours of my bedroom—the shoes lined up against the wall, the glare of the moonlight in the mirrored closet doors, the tall stack of books next to my bed. I picked up my phone: 4:05 a.m., only two hours past the last time I checked.

I'd had the dream again. For the last three weeks, I had not slept for more than two hours at a time. I'd been working eighteen-hour days for so long that all the days rolled together into one long day that never ended. I was being slowly crushed under the weight of worry and all the campaign tasks that remained undone. I could not turn off the clock inside my head, even at the end of the day when I needed rest. I would lie in bed, and in my mind, I would itemize the list of things I still needed to do. Behind those thoughts would be the sound of the clock reminding me that I could not catch up. *Tick-tick-tick.*

During the few hours that I slept each night, I had vivid dreams that I could fly. My body would lift from my bed and glide high above treetops and mountains, over oceans and rivers, soaring to places unknown. From my perch in the air, I would look down and see people far below me, and I would feel sad for them because they were stuck on the ground. Mostly, I would fly alone, peaceful and happy for what felt like an eternity. Then, at the moment when I was happiest, I would suddenly plummet back to earth. Boom! I woke up just before my body hit the ground, returned to my twin-size bed in my still-dark St. Louis apartment bedroom, usually only an hour or two after I had fallen to sleep. *Tick-tick-tick*, and the scene would begin again.

I got out of bed to splash some water on my face.

It was October 18, and yesterday had been a very good day.

Almost two months earlier, Lloyd and I had flown to DC to meet with the National Republican Senatorial Committee's political director. We'd been talking on the phone with Chris LaCivita at least once a week, often much more, but Lloyd had wanted to make our next appeal in person. We needed help. The eight-week, post–Labor Day blitz was only two weeks away, and everything we'd worked for over the past thirteen months would be put into play. It was the time frame during which our campaign would be won or lost.

Federal law prohibits Senate campaigns from coordinating too closely with entities like the NRSC, even though the sole reason for those entities' existence is to raise money to elect Republican candidates like Jim. We couldn't, for example, tell the NRSC that we needed them to drop a million dollars' worth of TV ads in the St. Louis area to appeal to women. We could, however, share poll results that highlighted weaknesses so they could deduce our strategy and help us on their own.

Next to Coddy, Chris LaCivita had become my closest ally and political friend. I considered him a political mastermind and loved watching him work. He could dissect an opponent's weakness with surgical precision, and he would patiently let the opponent twist in their own mistakes before going in for the kill—and he struck hard when he did. Two years later, in 2004, Chris would become the architect of the Swift Boat Veterans for Truth campaign that brought down presidential candidate Senator John Kerry, and in 2024, former President Trump asked Chris to run his campaign.

When Chris and I knew one another in 2002, I remember

thinking I had never been more grateful to have someone on my side (rather than the other way around). His takedowns of political opponents were legendary. He could also be uproariously funny, and being in a room with both him and Lloyd was comedic gold.

On that August day in DC, Lloyd and I walked into the NRSC conference room with Chris, and he told us that our race was at the top of his list for support. Lloyd and I looked at one another, relieved and joyful, knowing we'd made the right decision by visiting him in DC.

"Well, butter my butt and call me a biscuit!" Lloyd exclaimed. "That, sir, is darn good news."

"I thought you'd like that," Chris said. "Now, how can we help?"

Lloyd paused, as he so often did, for effect if nothing else. "Well, you know that Jean Carnahan is a grandmother, and a widow besides."

Chris nodded. "Yes, sir. I do."

Lloyd continued, "And you know that our candidate is a forty-six-year-old man who looks like he's a twenty-two-year-old nerd on a good day. Missourians don't want to see a widow and a grandmother get beat up by a young man. A male lawyer no less."

"Yes, sir," Chris said in solidarity.

"But Mrs. Carnahan, she's making all kinds of mistakes, and the voters have a right to know about them."

"They do, indeed," Chris agreed.

"But Jim can't be thrashing on her or coming off as too aggressive."

"Correct."

"Well, sir, that is the reason I'm here today. I wanted to express my thoughts on that." Having conveyed his message, Lloyd leaned back in his chair.

Chris's dark eyes bore into us like lasers, and he smiled. "Mark my words," he said. "Or, rather, mark your words, Lloyd."

Lloyd and I looked at one another before turning back to Chris, unsure of what he meant.

"We are gonna make Jean Carnahan madder than a sorry wet hen from the farmlands of Sikeston, Missouri, Lloyd. Just you watch."

Two months later, on October 15, Lloyd and I were—to use another Lloydism—smiling like pigs in shit. I'd gone into the week in a foul mood after coming back to my apartment late one night and noticing a piece of paper covering the keyhole of my front door. As I removed it from the handle, I realized it was a Jean Carnahan campaign flyer. On the front was a hideous picture of Jim, and on the back, my full name appeared alongside Jim's in a glossy font, with big lettering saying that a lawsuit had been filed against us for violating the law. I'd been expecting a hit piece like this since the Kraske article was published in March, and Lloyd had repeatedly warned me to be prepared. I thought I was. But seeing the flyer was like a kick to my stomach. Before walking inside, I looked at the doors of my neighbors' apartments. None of them had the flyer. Jean Carnahan's campaign obviously knew where I lived.

On Tuesday, October 15, Jean Carnahan was speaking at a Democratic luncheon that was being televised by CNN when she said, "I'm the number one target of the White House. They can't get Osama bin Laden, so they are going to get me."

Mrs. Carnahan said this, of course, because she was frustrated. President Bush had already come to Missouri three times to campaign for Jim, the equivalent of millions of dollars in television ads and maybe more. And, because of Coddy, the president had encouraged dozens of his administration officials to do the same. Our strategy to get as much earned media as possible was working, and Mrs. Carnahan was irritated.

To put her statement into meaningful context, Mrs. Carnahan uttered these words a mere two weeks after voting against the president's Homeland Security bill, during a campaign ad blitz claiming she lacked Jim's national security chops. Now, here she was, sounding like a victim while criticizing American troops for not having tracked down Osama bin Laden yet. Because CNN had recorded the lunch, the sound bite was extracted and played over and over on national news. Missourians were angry at her for mocking our brave American troops. Even so, she refused to apologize.

News media began calling our campaign office for Jim's response, and we weighed what to do, but we didn't need to think about it for very long. Because Jim was a forty-six-year-old man who couldn't beat up on a widow and a grandmother, our campaign sent out a short media statement rehashing her comments but declining to attack her for them. "I'm sure Mrs. Carnahan didn't mean to say what she said," we quoted Jim as saying. "And I'm sure most Missourians would accept a quick apology from her."

But the NRSC and the Missouri Republican Party weren't so forgiving, as we expected. They blasted her comment as "despicable." For twenty-four hours, Mrs. Carnahan's press secretary defensively shot back to the media that no apology would be forthcoming. The next day, Mrs. Carnahan apologized.

As I splashed water on my face that morning after waking up from my dream, I noticed myself smiling in the mirror. I looked at my face. Sleep-deprived. Devoid of healthy color. A stress pimple forming between my eyebrows. But I was smiling, and I felt sickened by my glee. What kind of person rejoices in another's downfall, even if the one falling is a campaign opponent who has done awful things to you?

A person in politics, that's who.

Sixteen more days.

WILD GEESE

October 2002 (Age 31)

By the middle of October, Jim had forgiven me for telling him I was moving to Australia no matter the outcome of the election. We never had another direct conversation about it, but small gestures communicated his hope for healing between us. He would buy me pecans from a country store on his travels. He'd go out of his way to thank me for my work on bringing so many special guests to Missouri. He'd email me a joke he'd heard. Our relationship was not the same as it had been before—it never would be again—but things between us were honest now, and honesty felt real.

At midnight on Sunday, October 27—nine days before Election Day—Jim called me while racing to the hospital. His beloved ninety-one-year-old father, Milton, had gone into cardiac arrest. Milton died a few hours later, and Jim was utterly distraught. Although he and his dad certainly didn't agree on everything—Milton, for example, was Jewish and Jim was a born-again evangelical Christian—Milton remained a source of deep strength for Jim throughout his life. In many ways, Jim idolized him.

A few hours later, early on Sunday morning, I got out of bed when it was still pitch-black outside. I wanted to get on the Queeny Park running trail at sunrise when I would have the best chance of being all alone.

October mornings were cool in St. Louis, and after putting on my running shorts and sports top, I threw on a long-sleeve shirt for good measure. My mind was so tired, and I was almost dizzy from exhaustion, but as soon as my yellow Nikes hit the dirt, my body came alive. The sun sat low in the sky, poking through the tree branches as I navigated the terrain. Through woods, across fields, around a small lake, and back into the woods, I ran. My long ponytail flapped against my shoulders as my feet connected with the ground. For nine miles (I always did the four-and-a-half-mile loop twice), my muscles burned, and my lungs felt like they were consuming fire. Rosey's *Dirty Child* album flowed through my headphones. That fall, I would listen to her bluesy vocals and push my legs so hard I wondered if I would hurt myself, but I never did.

Canada geese lived on the lake at Queeny Park. I passed them twice on my run, and I watched them. They floated serenely on top of the water until they suddenly began pumping their wings and paddling their feet to launch themselves like rockets overhead. Airborne, their brown wings flapped into the sky, going to a place I did not know and my eyes could not follow. I watched them disappear and wondered what it would feel like to be completely free.

Orange and red leaves from the sugar maples covered the ground, and across the lake, the thinning mass of colored leaves highlighted the transformation of the seasons. I wondered at change and all that had to die for new life to emerge. That morning, the sense of death felt blinding. But underneath the ground, where new things grow, I knew that life would continue to rise.

DEBATES

October 2002 (Age 31)

I was in the campaign office looking over documents to get ready for our debate prep session with Jim later that afternoon. Jim's first televised debate with Mrs. Carnahan was in one week, and Jim was now in hyperdrive. Known for his raw intelligence, incredible memory, and mastery of subjects that most people considered highly mundane, Jim was a skillful debater. In fact, he even looked like a debater with his glasses and scholarly expression. Our campaign debate sessions were intense, hours-long affairs, and Jim was a stickler about having a full understanding of the history and status of every regulation and policy about which the debate moderator might pose a question. This made him a dedicated, outstanding legislator and public servant. It also made him a total pain in the ass during these sessions because he was relentless.

Suddenly, I heard an *a-hem*, and I looked up to see Lloyd standing in my office doorway. When I saw him, I had a strange feeling that I had just been asleep, or maybe I had only been daydreaming. I experienced this sensation a lot toward the end of the campaign. There was only a gauzy veil between my days and nights, and I was always so exhausted I could never be entirely certain, which was almost like I was hallucinating.

Lloyd looked exasperated. He barreled into my office, closed my door, and sat down on my sofa. I looked at him rubbing his temples.

"Oh, Jen," he finally said. "I don't know if I can do this debate thing again with Jim. These debate prep sessions are like a plasma drip for policy wonks."

I laughed. It seemed that Lloyd and the New Jen were two entirely different creatures, but they agreed solidly on two things: (1) the importance of making sure Jim felt ready for his debate with Mrs. Carnahan, and (2) the excruciating nature of debate prep sessions.

I evaluated my present situation and decided to take pity on him. I told Lloyd I would handle that afternoon's session. His relief was palpable.

"God bless you, Miss Jen," he said, getting up to hug me.

Later that afternoon, Brett, Rich, and I were in Jim's office as we got started on our debate prep session. We had tried to rearrange the furniture so it resembled a debate stage, and we were marginally successful, even finding a bright light to shine on Jim as a stand-in for a spotlight. The room was cluttered, though, with books and papers resting in small piles on the floor and our laptops and Blackberries on the tables in front of us. Coffee mugs and Diet Coke cans already covered every surface, including Jim's makeshift podium and his office windowsills. A few candy wrappers were sprinkled on the tables.

Brett and Rich were playing the debate moderators, and I was playing Mrs. Carnahan, not because I was the only woman but because everyone knew I was the best at getting under Jim's skin. Knowing policy was essential, and that was Jim's forte, but so was being prepared to avoid the traps laid by your opponent. That's where I came in.

About ten minutes in, I was looking at my email when I got a message from Sam. I discreetly tried to read his email by pretending I was doing policy research on my Blackberry, but his message was quite long, and I couldn't concentrate. I briefly excused myself from the room.

Sam was writing to update me on his plans. He was in Africa, getting ready to start a scuba diving venture in the archipelago off the coast of Mozambique. Reading his email, I felt flattened by his stories of adventure and excitement, while I was stuck in a basement office with bad lighting conducting debate prep. I had made a firm commitment to never again let anyone or anything divert me from following my own path and goals. Now, that commitment was being challenged. What I wanted was to get on a plane to Africa that afternoon. But I had a commitment to Jim, and I was determined to stick to it through Election Day.

I walked back into Jim's office just as Rich was asking him a question about how the Environmental Protection Agency regulated farmland. I shook my head twice to get my mind out of the clouds. I had to get myself back into character and prepare my own answer as the pretend Mrs. Carnahan, hoping to rattle a few cages and make this afternoon's session time well spent.

CHAPTER 12

The Election

ST. CHARLES RALLY

November 4, 2002 (Age 31)

A week before Election Day, I was in my office talking on the phone with Coddy. I was so tired I could barely focus on our conversation.

"I have some incredible news for you, Chief."

"Hit me."

"President Bush wants to come back to Missouri. He wants to come to St. Charles."

"Come back to Missouri?" I said in disbelief, knowing it took weeks to orchestrate presidential events. "When?"

"On Monday. The day before the election."

I groaned, and Coddy heard. The news should have elated me. The president's visit to vote-rich St. Charles, a populous Republican stronghold on the outskirts of St. Louis, could make an enormous difference in inspiring people to go to the polls and vote for Jim on Election Day. But I was staring squarely at other facts as well. The St. Charles Arena held ten thousand people, and no one on our senior team had any spare time they could dedicate to pulling off a rally of that size, especially in six days. If we concentrated on the president's rally, our Get Out the Vote efforts in other critical regions might suffer. Not to mention that if we held a presidential rally that sucked, we would have egg on our faces with both the president and our voters, and the news media would report that we had failed.

But I had little choice, so I took a leap of faith.

"Coddy," I said with far more confidence than I felt, "we'll do it. Thank you for taking such good care of us."

"I knew that's what you would say," he said. "You're gonna win this thing, Chief. You'll see. Just seven more days."

"Six," I said, correcting him. "Not counting Election Day."

As soon as I hung up with Coddy, I took a deep breath and gave myself a pep talk.

Can you do this, Jen? I asked myself.

Yes, I think I can do this, I answered.

How? How can you do it?

I challenged myself to think clearly.

Just like every other thing I've done. By taking one step at a time.

I took another deep breath, and then I got to work. I called every Republican congressional chief of staff in Missouri, begging for help, and they delivered. Jason Van Eaton, Senator Bond's chief of staff, took a leave of absence and moved into my campaign office for a week. Miriam's team mobilized every volunteer in the region. We rented buses to bring people in from all corners of Missouri. We booked a Marriott Hotel ballroom to stage ticket distribution. By Sunday night, we had moved a remarkable 9,400 tickets.

On Monday morning, November 4, I arrived at the St. Charles Arena early, a few hours before the Secret Service opened the doors to the public. I did my rounds, making sure everything was in place. I saw Jason, my colleague from Senator

Bond's office, who had camped in my office with me all week, and we gave each other a hug. I put on my Secret Service pin and walked up to the arena's stage.

The arena was empty, and every one of my footsteps echoed loudly inside the stadium. I looked up into the indoor amphitheater, with seats rising high above me, and imagined what it would look like in three hours. President Bush and the First Lady would be on the stage under the bright lights, along with Jim and Brenda, and the crowd would be roaring and waving flags and signs to cheer on Jim.

Standing by myself on the stage, I thought, *I did this. I said I could do it, and I did it.* This was my fifth campaign event with President Bush, and I was proud like I always had been, but the pride felt different this time. In the past, I'd basked in the glow of what I had done under my own ingenuity and hard work. This time, the pride felt similar to how you feel when you give the perfect gift to someone you care about. Not selfish, and longer lasting.

I left the stage and took the back hallway to Jim's holding room, which was a locker room that had been converted into a lounge. Two comfortable wing chairs, a sofa, and a small refrigerator were positioned inside for his comfort. I shut the door behind me. It was so quiet in that still-empty space that it was almost jarring, and I sat down in a chair.

This is it, I thought. *My final presidential event, my last day before Election Day, and my last week ever working in politics.* I would be leaving St. Louis on Friday.

I had thought about this day for months, doing everything I could to conjure it into arriving and often believing it might never come. So many times, I'd felt sure I would not be able to survive until the end. My efforts had been squarely focused on reaching today, my last day, and here it was.

I did not feel joyful. I had never worked so hard for anything, and it was all about to end. I savored the moment of quiet and reflected on every square inch of the space—the buzzing refrigerator, the door, the tiny sofa, the shelves—and told myself to never forget any of it. Sitting in the wing chair, I pulled my knees to my chest and buried my face in them, but I did not cry. What I felt was more overwhelming than tears. It was the end of an entire life.

I had no thoughts about Australia in those moments. All of my focus was on what I was leaving behind. The job, the power, the position, all my hard work, Jim and Brenda, Lloyd, Coddy, my staff, the Secret Service, my dream of being a chief of staff in the Senate, the travel, long days and nights. I had wanted all of it for as long as I could remember, and this morning, it was time to say goodbye.

It felt very sad, this goodbye, and I could not make it seem right that I was really and truly at the very end. Then, there was a knock at the door. It was the Secret Service telling me that Jim had arrived. It was showtime.

Later that afternoon after the rally was over, I was in my office at the campaign headquarters when there was a frantic knock at my office door.

"Yes, come in," I said casually. There were always frantic knocks at my door. I'd learned that one of my most important jobs was maintaining calm no matter what I felt inside. If I did not get rattled, no one else did, either.

A volunteer who was answering phones walked in, and she looked like she'd seen a ghost.

"Jen," she stammered before regaining her countenance of excitement and shock. "Jen! Jen! Karl Rove from the White House is on the line for you. Karl Rove!"

In 2002, Karl Rove was the most well-known political adviser in the country as well as President Bush's right hand and confidant. In Republican circles, he was widely considered to be a mastermind. If you spent any time watching the TV news, you knew about Karl Rove. Clearly, this volunteer watched the TV news.

"Thank you," I said in a way that was much more laid-back than I felt. "Please put him through."

I picked up on the first ring when the call rang on my line.

"Hello," I said.

"This is the switchboard on Air Force One. Let me put you through to Mr. Rove."

"Jen?"

"Yes, Karl. How are you?" I had decided to call him by his first name like we were old friends.

"Jen, I just wanted to thank you for the outstanding rally in St. Charles today. You have done an incredible job for Jim, and I'm calling to thank you."

"I appreciate that, Karl. I'm proud of everything we have accomplished."

"I'm very proud of the campaign you guys have run. You guys are going to win tomorrow."

"From your lips to God's ears." I laughed.

"How's Jim?"

"He's holding up well," I said. "He feels good."

"He should. Great work, Jen. And thanks again."

I put down the phone, and ten people pushed their way into my office at the same time, including Lloyd. They wanted to hear what my new friend Karl had to say.

"Well, la-di-frickin'-da," Lloyd said with great flair. "It looks like Little Miss Jen is now best friends with Karl Rove."

That made everyone laugh, including me. I did not know it then, but in a few days' time, Karl Rove would ask Coddy to call me about postponing my plans for Australia.

ELECTION DAY

November 5, 2002 (Age 31)

Thirty hours after Karl Rove's call, at 12:40 a.m., forty minutes past Election Day, Lloyd and I were standing in the middle of a second-floor hallway in the Hilton St. Louis Frontenac. Hundreds of Jim's supporters were in the ballroom below, waiting for news about the election results. The polls had been closed for over five hours, but the race had remained too close to call. Jim and Brenda, along with their church's pastor and his wife, were in the presidential suite one floor above us, also waiting for news. They had turned the TV off in the suite, and Jim had said he did not want to hear any noise about the election. My instructions were to call him directly the moment I knew something definitive.

As Lloyd and I were talking, I looked down at my Blackberry. Jim was calling, but I did not know what to tell him, so I didn't pick up his call. This was cruel, really, because Jim knew that I would only ignore him if the news was not good. But, in fact, the news was not good. Lloyd and I decided it was best to tell him face-to-face.

All night, in almost every one of Missouri's 114 counties, votes for Jim had exceeded our projections, and Jim was well on track to win. At 11:00 p.m. on Election Night—four hours after the polls had closed—Jim had a three-point lead, and he kept climbing. Up 4 percent, then 5, and at midnight, he was leading by over eighty thousand votes, with about 67 percent of all votes being reported. But the two most important counties—the counties where the race would be decided, Democrat-leaning St. Louis County and Republican-leaning Greene County (where Springfield was located)—were lagging behind on reporting vote totals.

Just after 12:30 a.m., St. Louis County reported its returns. Our campaign's vote model had predicted that Jim would win

St. Louis County by over fifteen thousand votes. But when the returns came in, we learned that Jim would not win the county; in fact, he lost it by that same margin—about fifteen thousand votes. Our solid lead instantly evaporated. That was when Lloyd and I left our campaign's makeshift war room, the second-floor hotel conference room where vote totals were being called in by our campaign's precinct leaders around Missouri and crunched by our staff. We went out into the hall to talk privately.

"We've got to talk to Jim," Lloyd said. I was staring at my ringing phone as *Jim* flashed on the caller ID.

"What are we going to tell him?" I whispered, fear running through my veins.

"The truth," Lloyd said. "That's all we have."

We walked down the hall in silence, side by side. When we got in the elevator, Lloyd looked at me with water in the wells of his eyes. I reached down and squeezed his hand.

When we entered the presidential suite together, Jim looked alarmed. He and Brenda were sitting on the U-shaped sofa with their pastor and his wife next to them. All four of them remained seated when we came over to them, and Lloyd and I remained standing. Jim's face emanated panic, which he was working to cover with a slight smile, but I knew him too well. I knew he was dying inside.

"So, Jim, here's the deal," Lloyd said matter-of-factly. "The good news is that you're still in the lead, but only by about one percent."

"What's the bad news?" Jim asked.

"The bad news is that we got creamed in St. Louis County, and there is still ten percent of the vote left to be counted."

"What should we do? Should I go downstairs and make a statement?" Jim asked. His eyes were wide and looked wild, terrified of what looked to be inevitable.

"We're going to wait a little longer," Lloyd said calmly. "Then we will know."

For ten minutes, there was silence. No one in the room said anything, and not one person moved. Lloyd and I stood like centurions over the sofas, our eyes glued to our phones. Then, Lloyd's phone started to ring.

Everyone looked up at one another before all sets of eyes turned to Lloyd. He picked up his phone. "Hello. This is Lloyd."

It was Mrs. Carnahan's campaign manager, telling Lloyd that Mrs. Carnahan wanted to speak with Jim.

Lloyd put his phone over his chest so they could not hear us talking. "It's Jean," he said to Jim. "She wants to speak with you." Lloyd handed his phone to Jim.

"What should I say?" Jim whispered.

"Just talk to her," Lloyd quietly responded.

"Hello, Jean," Jim said into the phone. The world stopped. Everyone in the room stared at Jim. I stopped breathing.

"Thank you, Jean. You have run an incredible race, and it's been a privilege."

That was all that was said. Jim put down the phone. He looked at us in utter shock. Mrs. Carnahan had called Jim to concede the race. In the twenty minutes that Lloyd and I had been in the suite, the vote returns from Southwest Missouri, home to the city of Springfield and several counties, had come in. They pushed Jim into a solid lead with no pathway other than victory.

Brenda screamed. Lloyd bent over and started to weep. Jim walked over, hugged me, and didn't let go. He was sobbing. "I know what you've done for me, Jen. I know what you've given up for me. I will never forget that. Never." Brenda walked over to join us, and with Jim and Brenda's arms around my shoulders, I, too, started to cry.

It was the single most amazing moment of my entire life.

Jim Talent would be the next United States senator from the state of Missouri. Ten minutes later, he was on a stage in the hotel ballroom, illuminated by the massive lights from twenty live TV cameras broadcasting his words on news stations across the world. With Brenda at his side, he thanked his supporters for the victory. Lloyd and I stood next to them, and the hundreds of supporters who remained at the hotel cheered Jim on. It was past 3:00 a.m. when Jim finished his media interviews and left the hotel to go home.

I never went back to my apartment that night. I stayed in the presidential suite and drank champagne all night long. At 3:30 a.m., I kicked my heels off and danced in my bare feet to Eminem alongside a few campaign friends. We sang along to every word. I felt like I was flying.

Then dawn came, and it was over.

GOODBYES

November 6, 2002 (Age 31)

The next morning, I began moving out of my apartment, and on Thursday, two days after Election Day, I packed up my campaign office. This turned out to be one of the most emotionally excruciating things I'd ever had to do. Everything I touched held a memory—my huge map of Missouri with pins indicating Jim's travels; my big, handwritten sign declaring *Experience Matters!*, our campaign slogan; a photograph of Lloyd and myself at an American Legion dinner. As I put the items into a box, the collection almost floored me.

No one could believe I was leaving. Everyone thought I'd been hedging my bets to have a safety net in case we lost the campaign. At the end of the day, I gave myself thirty minutes to say goodbye to the staff—Miriam, Rich, and Brett most of all. My farewells were inappropriately brief, but had I allowed myself more time, I would not have been able to stay the course and leave. The lump in my throat felt like it was the size of a grapefruit when I hugged each of my battle-worn friends and said goodbye.

Coddy was the last person I spoke to on my campaign phone. He was calling to ask me if I was really moving to Australia.

"I am," I said to him. "But, Coddy, it is very difficult." I said this because I knew he would understand the depth of loss I felt and maybe provide some insight. I was having second thoughts.

"Karl asked me to call," he said. "We don't want you to go. We have a job for you at the White House, and I can make that happen ASAP."

I paused, dumbfounded. My mind raced, and I felt immediately tempted to give up all my plans and cave in. How could I say no to the White House, to *Coddy* of all people? I sat quietly, quickly thinking over his offer. I remembered the very first time he'd called me and my assumption that I'd ruined everything with the White House. Now, twelve months later, he was asking me to work with him. I beamed with a pride that nearly toppled my resolve.

"I've got to go to Australia, Coddy. But thank you. Thank you so much for everything you have done for me."

"Well, let me know if you change your mind. You know what my vote is. But thank you, Chief. You're awesome. Good luck."

I hung up the phone and unplugged it from the wall to prevent it from ringing again. If Coddy called back, I wasn't sure I would be as strong the second time.

The only time I cried was when saying goodbye to Lloyd. I told him I loved him like a big brother, and my heart overflowed with gratitude for him.

"You will always be my number one partner in crime," I said.

"I love you, too, Miss Jen. I never thought I'd say that to a fancy lawyer like yourself, but I sure as shit do, and that's the truth."

We hugged one another and did not let go for almost a minute. It was an awkwardly long time, and we knew it. I would profoundly miss him.

As I left the campaign office for the last time, I gripped my steering wheel so tightly that my fingers turned a shade of white, and I looked straight ahead at the road in front of me.

THE LAST SUPPER

November 2002 (Age 31)

Jim had arranged to have a celebratory dinner at one of St. Louis's finest restaurants, Dominic's on the Hill. The gesture meant so much to me, but I dreaded going. For fifteen months, Jim, Brenda, and I had shared a life together. When times were horrible, when we didn't know what the next day would bring, when we were mad at one another, when we were sharing the best moments possible—we had been through it all. How would I be able to say goodbye to the two people who had been my entire world?

When I walked into the restaurant, the maître d' asked me if I was joining Senator Talent's table, and there and then, my bottom lip began to quiver. Senator Talent. How long I'd waited to hear those words. I held in tears as he walked me to the restaurant's finest table, and Jim and Brenda stood when they saw me. My lips were still trembling.

Jim said, "There she is! Miss Blueberry!" And I lost it. Tears erupted from my eyes and rolled down my face, and I had to bend over because I was crying so hard. I picked up a napkin from the table and began wiping myself off. Brenda hugged me, and then Jim did. I felt their support, and it buoyed me. I hoped they could feel mine.

Jim's light and joyful mood sliced through my insides, and all the best parts of my life with him and Brenda came roaring back to the forefront. Over dinner, we howled with laughter for almost three hours, reminiscing about how many Diet Cokes we'd consumed, the plots of the dozen movies we had watched in their basement TV room, the Uno games we'd played and always lost to their son, and the long car and plane trips we'd endured for over a year to take us across the state and back. Jim reminded me of the afternoon we'd spent at the Galleria mall fifteen months before, in August 2001, when I'd "commanded him"—his words, not mine—to get new eyeglasses. He said I'd called his glasses "dorky."

"We could have saved ourselves a whole lot of worry and effort," Jim said while laughing hysterically, "if we'd only realized then that my new glasses would win us this race."

Brenda was laughing, too. "Well, *obviously*," she said. "You no longer looked like a dork."

In all of my life, before or since, I have never enjoyed three hours more than I enjoyed my time at dinner that night.

We said our goodbyes on the street outside Dominic's as I was opening my car door. We hugged and told one another we'd email soon. Our parting looked no different that night than it had on any of the dozens of times I'd left their house after dinner with the taste of cheesecake still in my mouth. A passerby might have expected that I would see them the next day. This goodbye worked best because getting too sad would have opened the emotional floodgates for all of us. As I pulled away from the curb, I looked in my rear-view mirror and watched Jim and Brenda turn and walk away.

Part Two

Rewired

CHAPTER 13

Alternative Endings

STORYLINES

March 2003 (Age 31)

One afternoon, I was ambling along High Street in Prahran, Melbourne, when I came upon a lovely shop with white-washed walls and Victorian iron scrolling. The building was similar to many of the old buildings in Melbourne. It had a small wooden sign out front: PETER ARNOLD RARE BOOKS. I walked inside.

The experience of moving to Melbourne had been like becoming a child again. Australians and Americans both speak English, but, as far as I could see, the similarities ended there. Every day was an adventure and filled me with surprise at how different things were here than in the United States. From vegetation to architecture to the small shops and pubs that lined nearly every street, Melbourne was an education.

I circled the stacks of books at Peter Arnold's antiquarian bookshop until I found it: an early edition hardback copy of *The French Lieutenant's Woman.* I'd read Sam's ratty paperback version from cover to cover three times, and I thought this beautiful old edition would be a perfect gift for him. I loved the story for its hauntingly romantic quality and the way it bent time and space around the main characters. But on that day in the rare-book shop, I didn't understand the main point of the story, not really. It wasn't until many years later that I did.

The French Lieutenant's Woman is a tale about alternative endings. Set in the nineteenth century, the book's main characters are star-crossed lovers who live out their lives in three alternative ways with profoundly varying conclusions—all of which are revealed in the book. The reader knows this is happening because the narrator himself enters the story and chooses each unique ending by flipping a coin.

I have wondered many times if Sam's book gift was prophetic, and although I'm not suggesting it was, I'm not saying it wasn't, either. When I read political news, I nearly always see a reference to someone I know from my political days, prompting me to ask questions about my own past and the choices I have made. Is there a connection between the book's storyline and the life I have lived? Had my own coin toss landed with heads up instead of tails, or if I had made other choices—well, I probably wouldn't be telling this story. Likely, I'd be working alongside my former friends and colleagues to support President Trump. Or Ron DeSantis. Or Kanye West. Or Josh Hawley. In any scenario, I certainly wouldn't be living in California.

I have lived with questions about alternate endings for the better part of twenty years now. One thing I've learned is that none of us can ever truly escape our pasts. The key, I think, is coming to terms with the past while learning to carry both pain and a hope of redemption. This is the work that transforms us, even if we don't quite understand the reasons why.

THE FEARLESS, SYDNEY, AUSTRALIA

December 26, 2002 (Age 31)

Almost a month after I'd been living in Australia, the alarm on my Australian Vodafone started ringing at 6:00 a.m., and I shot up in bed. It was Boxing Day, and the Sydney to Hobart Sailing Race would start in seven hours. I'd been waiting for this day since I'd read *The Proving Ground.* Today was the day.

My body was humming. I threw off my covers and got out of bed. To stretch my money as far as possible, I was staying above a restaurant in a meager room for rent during my five days in Sydney. I had my own room, but I shared a bathroom with other guests, so I got dressed before going across the hall to wash my face. The place was sparse, but it was clean. Most importantly, it was just a few steps away from Sydney Harbour.

I'd been in Sydney for four days already, plenty of time to research the best way to view the start of the race. I'd asked everyone I met for their advice: people at Sydney's Visitor's Center, people at the ferry port on Circular Quay, people in pubs and restaurants, and people who worked near the harbor. "From a boat" was the universal consensus on the best place to watch the race. Apparently, massive cordoned-off areas along the shoreline were set up for pleasure boaters to view the competing maxi yachts. Unfortunately, I didn't know anyone in Sydney, much less anyone who owned a boat.

"That sounds fantastic," I'd told the throngs of people who'd answered my question this way. "But where's the best spot to watch the race from the shore?"

North Head State Park was the answer. This was the swath of land at the northernmost edge of the harbor before the boats raced out into the Tasman Sea. From just behind the Opera

House, the area where I was staying, it would take a ferry ride and a bus to get there. I had to start early.

The day was overcast and threatened rain. I threw on my jeans and a sweatshirt and shoved an umbrella into my backpack before walking to the Circular Quay. I caught one of the first ferries across the harbor to Manly Beach, then walked across the street to the coffee shop where I'd wait for my bus to the North Head. I ordered a latte and sat outside under the coffee shop's awning.

Two Australian men were sitting at the table adjacent to mine, and one of them had an adorable little dog who kept coming over to play with me.

"What a cute dog!" I said as I reached over to pet him.

"He's not as cute as he looks," one of the men said. He looked like he was a few years older than me and was casually gorgeous in the way that so many Australian men are, as if he lived on the beach without a care in the world. "Where are you from?" He'd obviously detected my American accent.

I had to think about this and decided DC would be more recognizable than St. Louis. Anyway, I wasn't from St. Louis anymore. I wasn't really from anywhere, come to think of it.

"I'm American," I said. "From Washington, DC."

"What is a girl from Washington, DC, doing in Manly on a rainy morning like this?"

"I've traveled to Sydney to see the race today," I said to him. "I've been so excited to see it for a long time now. I'm just waiting for the bus to take me up to North Head."

"Bonza!" he shouted, so loudly it startled me. "You're going to sit outside when it's pissing down rain just to watch the race?" He said this with disbelief, looking at me as if I weren't the sort of girl who would be so inclined.

"Absolutely!" I exclaimed. "I can't wait."

The two men looked at one another. Then the owner of the dog turned back toward me and said to his friend, "Whaddya think, mate? I think this girl deserves a Christmas pressie, don't you?"

It turns out that the man I'd been talking to, the handsome one with the cute dog, was a charter boat captain. Some members of the Australian news media had hired him for the day to take them out in his boat so they could cover the race. His name was JP, and he asked me if I'd like to come along.

My mouth fell open. "Oh my god," I said, stunned by the unexpected, unbelievable offer. "I'd love to!"

"C'mon then," JP replied. "Let's go."

His boat was called *The Fearless*. It was a forty-one-foot-long fishing boat with a massive flying bridge, a large deck, and a good-sized cabin with seating and a small kitchen. *The Fearless* flew the official Rolex racing flag from its tallest pole, indicating its status as an approved media boat. With JP at the helm, we picked up journalists from *The Sydney Morning Herald*, *The Australian*, and the Associated Press at the yacht club and drove the boat into the middle of the harbor. As we motored past the hundreds of pleasure boats watching the race from approved viewing spots near the shoreline, I kept pinching myself. *How is this amazing thing actually happening to me?!*

The ten-minute warning shot was fired at 12:50 p.m., and it startled me so badly I lost my balance. At 12:59 p.m., there was the one-minute-left-to-go warning signal. JP's first mate began screaming out the countdown in the last twenty seconds: "Twenty. Nineteen. Eighteen." As soon as he got to one, it was 1:00 p.m. and the starting gun fired. *The Fearless* was only a few meters in front of the biggest maxi yachts, which I'd read about for months in *The Proving Ground*: *Alfa Romeo*, *Brindabella*, *Cannon*. JP quickly pushed the throttle, and we shot out ahead of the boats and through the harbor's North and South Heads before we reached the open sea.

For two hours, I stood to one side of the flying bridge to stay out of JP's way. The weather conditions had turned from bad to worse, and JP was concentrating on getting close enough to the racing sailboats for the photographers to get the shots they needed. Accomplishing this while staying out of the maxi yachts' way was extremely difficult, complicated by the overcast weather. I could not make it seem right that I was there. How had I been so lucky as to walk into that coffee shop at exactly the time I did and sit down one table away from JP?

As the maxi yacht race leaders turned south toward Tasmania, the pouring rain made it difficult to see even a few meters in front of us, but I did not go inside the cabin. I let the rain pelt my body until I was no less wet than if I'd jumped into the Tasman Sea.

When the journalists told JP they had captured all the photographs they needed, we turned back toward the yacht club. I was at a loss for words while saying goodbye to JP. What could I possibly say to express how much the day had meant to me? Where would I even begin?

I gave him a hug and told him that today had been one of the most important days of my entire life. "Thank you, JP, from the bottom of my heart. Truly."

He smiled at me and put his hand on top of mine.

"A few years ago, when I was traveling through Europe, I had someone do something for me that was a life-changer, too," JP said wistfully. "I vowed I would pay it forward, and today, I had my chance. Thank you for letting me do that for you."

I put on the warmest sweatshirt I could find in my bag and left his boat. I would never see him again. On my final night in Sydney, I took myself out for a cup of coffee to celebrate.

CHAPTER 14

White Privilege

SOUTH SIDE OF CHICAGO

1960s (Before I Was Born)

I grew up in the suburbs, but I visited downtown Chicago dozens of times when I was a child, of course. At Christmastime, we'd pile into our green Volvo station wagon to visit the flagship Marshall Field's store on North Michigan Avenue, where we'd take photographs with Santa and buy boxes of Frango mints. Every summer, my mom would take my brother and me to Shedd Aquarium and the Field Museum. And on many Sundays after church, and every Easter without fail, our family would eat brunch behind the tall iron gates of the Beverly Country Club, where my grandparents were members.

Beverly, a neighborhood on the South Side of Chicago, is the place where both my mom and dad were born and raised. Their houses were only a few streets apart, and my parents had known each other since childhood. They both went to elementary, middle, and high school in Beverly—my mom at the public school and my dad at the private Morgan Park Academy.

On a lark after eating at the country club one Sunday, my parents thought it would be fun to show my brother and me the houses they'd grown up in. I was seven years old. They drove straight there, and the four of us pulled up to a cute gold brick bungalow on Leavitt Street.

"This is my old house," my mom said wistfully. I reached for the door handle so I could go outside.

"No." My mom turned toward me in the back seat, shaking her head. "It's different here now than when I grew up."

I sat back in my seat, confused. Leavitt Street didn't have large, beautiful houses and perfect lawns like Hinsdale, but it didn't look threatening. I was only seven, though, and already bored, so it didn't much matter to me one way or the other. As my dad drove away, I didn't know that I would never come back here again—but even if I had, I wouldn't have cared.

When every person on both sides of a family—in my case, four grandparents, five aunts and uncles, two cousins, and my parents—uproots entirely and leaves their community behind, there must be a story. The story I later heard was that my grandmother had been sitting in the front room of her house on Leavitt Street when she saw a young Black woman walk by on the sidewalk pushing a stroller. By all accounts, the woman was not rude or causing a disturbance; she looked like any young mother walking her child. But the point was that she was a young *Black* mother, which meant she might have more young babies at home to play with other Black children in the neighborhood. By then, my grandmother had seen many Black families move to Beverly. Her own friends had moved out, and property values fell. Within four years, my entire family had moved to Hinsdale, where I was born in 1971.

WANTING TO BE SOUTHERN

(Age 14 Onward)

As a Northerner, it was easy to get sucked into the warmth and gentility of Southern culture. Within months of moving to Richmond as a teenager, I was wearing floral Laura Ashley dresses with big pink-and-yellow bows in my long hair, and, in time, I developed a thick Southern accent, my speech filled with "y'alls" and phrases like "fixin' to" and "might could." I memorized the lyrics to songs by Lynyrd Skynyrd, Creedence Clearwater Revival, and Crosby, Stills and Nash. These changes were not add-ons to my personality but complete overhauls; I abandoned the girl who had existed before in favor of the updated *Steel Magnolias* version. I had moved so often that I desperately yearned to fit in. I wanted people to like me. But even more than that, I wanted *these people* to like me. Southerners seemed to me like the most fascinating people in the world.

I became obsessed with being Southern. During my first year of college, I immersed myself in Civil War history. I wrote papers about Mary Boykin Chesnut, the Confederate diarist from South Carolina. I interned at the White House of the Confederacy in Richmond and at the Alexandria Archaeology Museum, where I participated in an archaeological dig at the Fort Ward Civil War site in Northern Virginia.

When, on occasion, people suggested that I might be a Southern sympathizer—the South's genteel code word for *racist*—I could always convincingly answer in the negative. "Heavens, no," I'd reply. "I know it doesn't sound like it, but I'm from *the North*. I was born on Grant Street—you know, *Grant* Street, for Union General Ulysses S. Grant. In *Chicago*."

"I see," they'd reply. "You're from *Chicago*. Sorry for the mistake."

"Well, bless your heart," I'd say. And with that, the subject would be put to bed.

I loved the South, but in my own mind, I considered my hometown of Chicago to have been the land of the free and the home of the brave, free of the South's Jim Crow–supporting racists. To me and the others in my white, deeply Christian family, the rest was history. Ancient history. And that had always been the end of that.

AUCTIONS

1990 (Age 18)

In 1989, I graduated from the most exclusive private high school in Richmond before matriculating into a private liberal arts college for Christian Scientists. Principia College sat high on the bluffs overlooking the Mississippi River with a campus resembling the English countryside during the Renaissance. Designed by renowned architect Bernard Maybeck, a protégé of Frank Lloyd Wright, Principia's residence halls look like massive Tudor mansions. They dot grassy knolls with chapels and beautiful academic buildings sprinkled on the landscape. Both of my parents, two of my aunts, one of my uncles, and two cousins also attended Principia.

My residence hall was named Anderson West. Of the sixty or so women who lived there, as far as I know, only one was Black. Her name was Shauna, and within a few weeks of starting college, I became acutely aware that she did not like me. Bubbly and popular, I usually found that *everyone* liked me, but not Shauna. I made a few feeble attempts to win her over before I gave up.

White Privilege

In the spring of my first year, the residents of Anderson West were trying to decide on a fundraising idea for raising money to host a dinner dance. One night, all the women gathered in the living room to discuss it. In high school, I'd participated in many successful fundraisers for social clubs and other groups and considered myself somewhat of an expert on the subject. When it was my turn to speak, I suggested an idea.

"In high school, one of my clubs raised over a thousand dollars in one afternoon by having an auction," I said with great authority. "Each of us went up onstage one at a time, and the auctioneer read off the list of chores that we agreed to do. Some of us said things like 'Help with your homework' or 'Make a picnic lunch.' You can also say things like 'I'll clean your room' or 'I'll do your laundry.'"

I could tell by the way the women were leaning in and nodding that they loved the idea, so I kept going.

"It was really fun. We painted huge signs to promote the fundraiser and held the auction in the dining hall during lunch so everybody would be in one place to bid on us."

From the back of the room, one of the seniors said, "That's a great idea, Jen. What did you call it?"

"We called it Rent-a-Slave," I said cheerfully. "And each of us numbered ourselves. You know, Slave Number One, Slave Number Two, like that."

The chatter continued until Shauna stood up and pointed a finger at me. "I will absolutely not participate in anything called Rent-a-Slave."

"Why not?" I looked in her direction and felt embarrassed for her. She was making a scene.

"Isn't it obvious?" she yelled. "It's glorifying slavery!"

"Oh, *come on*," I said, rolling my eyes. "Get over it, Shauna.

Slavery hasn't been around for a very long time. No one is suggesting we will actually *be slaves*. We're just having a little fun."

Shauna looked at me in horror before storming out of the living room.

In the end, two seniors brokered a compromise. We held "Rent-a-Westie" ("Westie" for Anderson West) in the dining hall a few weeks later and raised thousands of dollars. I thought the name was dumb but joined in anyway. My future husband, John, spent the most to bid on me—$150. Shauna declined to participate.

MISSOURI WALTZ

June 2002 (Age 30)

The last time I sang the Missouri state song, "The Missouri Waltz," was at the American Legion Hall in Joplin, Missouri, in June 2002, four months before Election Day on the campaign.

The lyrics refer to dreaming of and returning to Dixie—the nickname for the states south of the Mason-Dixon Line that seceded and formed the Confederacy during the Civil War. This is considered the "non-racist" version of the Missouri state song (these lyrics came into use in 1949 because the original lyrics were even worse):

Way down in Missouri where I heard this melody,
When I was a Pickaninny on ma Mammy's knee;
The darkies were hummin'; their banjos were strummin';
So sweet and low. Hush-a-bye ma baby,
go to sleep on Mammy's knee,
Journey back to Dixieland in dreams again with me;
It seems like your Mammy was there once again,
And the darkies were strummin' that same old refrain.

If you want to hear the melody of "The Missouri Waltz," just tune in to any Mizzou football game. It's a standard song the Marching Mizzou—the University of Missouri marching band—plays at every game.

FERGUSON

August 9, 2014 (Age 42)

Almost twelve years after the campaign had ended, eighteen-year-old Michael Brown was killed by a white police officer in Ferguson, Missouri, on the second Saturday in August 2014. His dead body was left uncovered in the street to bake in the hot sun for over four hours. I learned this that night by watching the TV news from my house in Richmond.

Michael had been shot on Canfield Drive, which was about seven miles from our Talent for Senate headquarters on Olive Boulevard. Even though twelve years had passed, I could still see the Missouri map on my office wall with the hundreds of push-pins identifying our campaign's travels around the state. The map had long since been thrown away, but I knew for certain that there had been no pin along Canfield Drive. I don't think there had been a pin for Ferguson, either.

In our fifteen months on the campaign trail, I had personally driven the four-and-a-half-hour trek across the state to Joplin, Missouri, four times. Joplin's most famous son may have been poet Langston Hughes, but in 2002, the city was 80 percent white and voted overwhelmingly Republican. To win the Senate, Jim needed to—and did—win Joplin by a landslide. Similarly, I'd been to Springfield five times, along with Poplar Bluff, Sullivan, Tarkio, and St. Joseph. Jim and I had also visited St. Charles, a bastion of Republican voters twelve miles from our St. Louis office, more times than I could count.

Ferguson, on the other hand, was almost 70 percent African American with a poverty level twice the national average. I guessed that not even Jean Carnahan had been to Ferguson in 2002. The city had been completely ignored.

When Michael was shot in 2014, I watched the riots unfold from my television set in Richmond. Hundreds of faces raged in the darkness as people shouted, chanted, cried. Fires burned on the perimeter of the television screen, emitting a glow from inside the broken windows of buildings and burning cars. What stopped me cold were the protesters' fuming eyes. In truth, their eyes scared me, but I did not turn away from them. I was beginning to glimpse what it meant to occupy the safe space claimed by the fragility of white women who were waking up to truths so big they cannot be clearly understood. The pain I felt was not fabricated, but it was not real, either, for loss of entitlement is not a thing to be mourned. In some way, I sensed this even as I felt it.

As I watched TV, I saw police officers clash with Black and brown faces in the streets of Ferguson, but I could not see the officers' eyes. They were hidden behind face shields and body armor. Some of the officers rode inside tactical vehicles that resembled tanks. It occurred to me that had I been able to see their faces, I might have recognized some of them. Even though twelve years had passed, I'd worked closely with many police officers on the campaign trail. I couldn't see their eyes, but I could see their hands on holsters carrying firearms and nightsticks. Some of them held leashes attached to German shepherds.

As the buildings and businesses in Ferguson burned, I had a glimpse of understanding for the very first time. For twelve years and twenty years and hundreds of years, all the way back to the time when Black bodies were beaten and raped and stolen from their homes and carried across the Atlantic as cargo and sold at auctions as slaves to white people all across the Southern United States, white people have failed to listen. We don't listen because not listening means we can maintain the systems that protect our white money, lifestyles, and power. Listening would force us to consider change.

If we do not listen, we can act surprised and angry when buildings burn.

We can ask with all the sincerity in the world, "Why do *they* do that?" and label Black protest as vandalism.

I know this because it is what I used to do.

CORPORAL JACAI COLSON

March 13, 2016 (Age 42)

In 2014, I started a new job working as the chief of staff for the president of a historic liberal arts institution, and two years later, I attended a three-day political speechwriting conference in Washington, DC. As chief of staff, I served as my president's speechwriter, just like I'd served as Jim's speechwriter years earlier. I hoped the conference would sharpen my skills.

There were many excellent talks at the conference focusing on craft, theme selection, and how to make speeches resonate. But the most impactful presentation occurred on the second day of the conference. President Clinton's former speechwriter spoke about how love—yes, *love*—can serve as the basis for the speeches we write to transform our audiences and our own souls. It seemed like a strange topic, but by the end of his remarks, I was in tears, literally holding back heaving sobs in a room full of hundreds of people. As he finished, I excused myself from my table to go to the bathroom so I could finish my crying and clean myself up.

As part of his sixty-minute talk, the presenter showed clips from TED Talks to amplify his meaning. The longest one was from a TED Talk by a person I'd never heard of before, a man named Bryan Stevenson. A Harvard-educated lawyer, his grandmother had been the daughter of people who were enslaved in Virginia. He now headed the Equal Justice Initiative, a nonprofit organization in Alabama working to end mass incarceration and racial inequality. His statistics about incarceration rates for Black males were staggering, as were his examples of the astounding racial and socioeconomic inequality in the criminal justice system. I learned more in twenty minutes than I had in a lifetime. I wondered, *How could I not have known any of this before?* He communicated these shocking truths by couching them inside magnificent language about the power of identity and forgiveness—and love—and it brought me to my knees. "Each of us is more than the worst thing we've ever done," he said, and few things I have ever heard in my life have pierced my heart like those words did. On my two-hour drive back to Richmond the next day, I listened to Bryan Stevenson's TED Talk the entire way, hitting "replay" over and over and over again. His words cut me like thorns because I had been so woefully ignorant and devastatingly blind, but they were a balm, too. A sense of promise rose in me that I could do better as a white woman, *would* do better, to understand my own racism, work to become an anti-racist person, and further racial and social justice where I could. That afternoon, I vowed I would try.

One week later, a young Black detective from the Prince George's County Police Department was gunned down in the line of duty outside his police station in Maryland. His name was Officer Jacai Colson, and he was only twenty-eight years old. His death was senseless and tragic, and he was mourned around the United States, including at the college where I worked. Jacai was a Randolph-Macon College graduate, class of 2009.

The very first speech I wrote following the speechwriting

conference in Washington, DC, was a eulogy to mourn Corporal Jacai Colson. The college's president would read it at a candlelight vigil on our campus. I prayed before I started writing, focusing on my desire to channel both love and what I had learned from Bryan Stevenson. I wrote it in a record-breaking one hour—a first. When I finished, I gave it to the college president and watched him read it from across his large wooden desk. Near the end of my speech, when he read these lines, he himself started to weep:

> As I was thinking through what I would say here tonight, I was reminded of something Eleanor Roosevelt said: "We do not become heroes overnight. Just a step at a time, meeting each thing that comes up . . . discovering we have the strength to stare it down."
>
> And I believe that this is what is being asked of us as we consider whether there could be any possible meaning in the tragic loss of Jacai.
>
> We look into our own hearts and say, "Today, I can do better. I can be more kind. More committed. More selfless. I can care for my community just a little bit more than I did this morning. I can be a little less hesitant and a little more bold in my own call, just like Jacai was."

When the college president read my speech at the candlelight vigil before hundreds of faculty members, staff, and students, his eyes once again welled up with tears. I had never known Jacai, but as I listened, I cried, too. I realized that in memorializing Jacai's meaningful life, my words also served as a letter to myself, reminding me of who I was. Somehow, in writing Jacai's eulogy, my most powerful demons of shame and regret had loosened, and I began to heal.

BECOMING BY MICHELLE OBAMA

November 2018 (Age 47)

Ana's gray Honda CR-V climbed up the steep, open highway, and the furry green tips of the dense Oregon pine forest stretched above us. It was November, four days after Thanksgiving, and snow sat on the ground in thick clumps, edging the road. I, the one visiting, rode shotgun. Ana drove.

I looked over at her behind the wheel. Ana was beautiful. With brown skin and the svelteness of a yoga instructor, she imbued equal parts wildness and discipline. She intrigued me endlessly, which is to say I was a little bit envious of her. We both worked in higher education; she was a professor at a large public university, and I was a chief of staff at a small private college. We'd known each other since 2010, when both of us were pregnant at the same time—Ana with her first child and me with my youngest son, Michael, who, coincidentally, I named after Ana's husband.

We have always gotten along well, Ana and I. Mostly, this is because I make her laugh, and she considers me to be a bit crazy. For example, as we drove from Corvallis to the Oregon Coast, I'd downed three Diet Cokes in the space of an hour and had to go to the bathroom *again*. I knew this news would annoy her, given that we'd already stopped once and still had a few more hours to go until we reached Cannon Beach. Also, she believes my constant Diet Coke consumption is totally gross, given that she only drinks things like kombucha and matcha green tea—two beverages I wouldn't be caught dead drinking. So, I artfully couched my news about needing to pee.

"Okay, look," I said. "The bad news is that I need to go to the bathroom again, so you're going to have to stop. The good news is that I agree to wearing adult diapers for the rest of the journey."

This made her laugh, but not as much as when I met her at the gas station counter after having relieved myself in the ladies' room at Wanker's Country Store and slapped down a box of Depends on the countertop.

The other reason Ana likes me is that we easily fall into deep, important conversations. Ana is from Panama and was born to a Black Panamanian father and a white English mother. Her stories about growing up in Panama fascinate me to no end. She, in turn, is amazed by the fact that I used to be a conservative Republican. She didn't know me then, and I thank God for that. She always has a hard time envisioning the woman I was in those days and asks me a lot of questions. Her perennial favorite is how it is possible that someone like the present-day me could have been the woman I have described myself as back then. I've done my best to answer.

When we were back inside her car after the bathroom break, I reached into my handbag and pulled out the little marble notebook I carry with me everywhere. I use it to write down ideas or a phrase that's caught my eye. One marvelous byproduct of writing speeches again is that I've regained my childhood devotion to poetry, so the pages of my notebook are also scribbled with poems I love. Oliver, Rilke, O'Donohue, Angelou, Whyte, Wiman, Palmer, Hughes. I randomly flipped to a page where I'd copied a poem by the Arab American poet Naomi Shihab Nye, "Kindness." I love this poem so much that I'd recently memorized it, and I asked Ana if she'd heard of it.

"No," she said.

"Shall I read it?"

Ana nodded.

The part of the poem that caught her breath is the stanza that catches everyone's breath. It's about an Indian in a white poncho who lies dead along the roadside. Nye writes so beautifully about how important it is to recognize that he could be any of us. And she reminds us that kindness goes hand in hand with sorrow.

"How beautiful," Ana said. And I nodded.

As we drove west, the sky was gray and misty, and droplets of rain covered the windshield. The car summited a mountain crest, and the open Cascade Mountain vistas appeared wide before us. I realized I had not drawn breath during the climb upward; I was so in awe of the beauty that I let out a large sigh.

On the next page of my notebook, I'd written notes from Oprah's interview with Michelle Obama in which Obama talked about her new book, *Becoming*. Ana loved Michelle Obama, and I knew this. I'd read the book from cover to cover during the past few days in anticipation of my Thanksgiving trip to Oregon, even though it had only been out for a few weeks. I asked Ana if she'd read it yet.

"Just starting," she said. "What did you think?"

"You remember I never voted for Obama," I said, not answering her question.

Ana sighed. "Yes, I know," she said. She simply couldn't reconcile Before Jen with Now Jen, and I couldn't blame her. In the past, I'd shared with her that as I'd watched a televised Barack Obama give the keynote speech at the 2004 Democratic National Convention in Boston, I'd been poised to dislike him as an unqualified upstart. But as I listened, I'd grown so engrossed in what he was saying that I forgot to take my boiling spaghetti off my stove for over an hour, long after it became a mushy mess. "*E pluribus unum*," Obama had said, raising the inflection of his voice, like a gifted preacher. I'd quickly written down those three Latin words with a Sharpie on a piece of paper towel in my Washington, DC, kitchen. "Out of many, one." I loved that phrase and wanted to remember it.

But when Obama ran for president four years later, I'd been disabused of any desire I'd ever had to like him. Every night while preparing dinner for my then toddler, Jack, I'd listen to Glenn Beck and Sean Hannity on Fox Radio talking about the Obamas' anti-American ways. I'd been particularly outraged by the statements of their Black pastor, Reverend Jeremiah Wright, about America deserving what happened on 9/11. As Beck and Hannity drove those comments home by ripping them apart for hours every night, I became more and more disturbed by what I was hearing about Barack Obama.

It wasn't until after Michael Brown was killed in Ferguson, Missouri, and I became familiar with the work of Bryan Stevenson and others like him that I began to see through the lies and change my mind about the Obamas. But that transformation happened too late for me to vote for him in a presidential race. Since 2015, however, I have not voted for any Republican for any office. Ana knew this, too.

I told her how much I loved *Becoming* and said I was moved by Michelle Obama's skillful recounting of white flight's impact on the South Side of Chicago, including her own classroom photographs, which showed, in literal black-and-white, its impact on the schools. Early in her elementary school career, her photographs showed a mix of Black and white students in her classes; later on, the students were overwhelmingly Black.

"My own family was part of the problem," I told her. "We were from the South Side, too, but in 1970, my family moved out, and I was born in a suburb."

Ana looked surprised. We'd not discussed this before.

I continued. "The way Michelle Obama talks about this fills me with so much shame about what I didn't understand and didn't want to understand."

Ana gripped the steering wheel as she listened, then looked over at me like the professor she was. "How is it possible for a human being to change as much as you have?"

I paused. She'd asked me this several times before.

"Pain," I said. "Like the poem. I was in so much pain, I had to learn what it meant to love. And how to listen."

WOKE

July 2020 (Age 49)

I can hear one of my good friends saying it now: "You're woke, Jen! What the hell happened to you?!"

Six months before my family moved to California, I encouraged our two sons—both youth soccer players—to run laps to raise money and awareness for Black Lives Matter in the wake of George Floyd's murder. They were twelve and ten years old at the time, and running was something they knew how to do. They successfully raised $700 despite the fact that none of our closest friends donated even one dollar to their cause. When they made a sign boasting about their accomplishment, we took a picture and posted it on social media. The friend who called me woke, a former US Navy and commercial pilot, never lets an opportunity to praise Donald Trump or his policies pass him by. For example, he once posted that the earthquake striking New York City in April 2024 was God's response to the district attorneys prosecuting Trump. He also wrote that California is the front door of Hades. I felt tempted to acknowledge his posts with a few fire emojis but held back.

When we posted about our sons supporting Black Lives Matter and George Floyd, he chastised us for not using the opportunity to talk about the bravery of police officers. I did not engage. I've learned the hard way that discretion is the better part of valor when it comes to social media.

People like my friend are proud to proclaim themselves anti-woke, which is such a strange phrase to me. Doesn't that mean that they are sleeping?

QUINCEAÑERA

April 2024 (Age 52)

At the university where I now work in Southern California, the columned administration building stands on a hill, and its tall steps offer a stunning view of the surrounding mountains and our gorgeous campus below. Every day, and usually many times a day, fifteen-year-old girls wearing brilliantly colored dresses with enormous hoop skirts line up on our steps to take photographs for their quinceañeras, and today was no exception. I waited at the bottom until the photographer waved me through, and I made a wide berth around the girl's purple-blue skirt as I climbed the stairs.

"You look beautiful," I said. "I love your dress."

"Thank you," she said, fluttering her eyelashes as she smiled. She tossed her long black hair over her shoulder in preparation for the photographer's next click. She did look beautiful, and she knew it.

Our university was founded in 1907 and has served as a residential liberal arts campus for many decades. Indeed, it still does, although many things have changed. We are now a Hispanic-Serving Institution, or HSI, a United States Department of Education designation for colleges and universities where over 25 percent of undergraduate students are of Latinx descent. The university offers a Native Students program, partnering with the nearby Yuhaaviatam of San Manuel to encourage

Native students to attend college and then support them once they arrive. Powwows with massive attendance by tribal peoples from around the United States are held on our campus, as is one of the largest Juneteenth celebrations in our region. One of our newest and most popular cocurricular offerings is a mariachi ensemble. Another is Hawaiian dance.

I am still learning about what it means to be anti-racist. Nearly every week, I am reminded that some phrase I've used for my entire life or a culturally conditioned value I have internalized has the underpinnings of racism, and I am trying hard to do better, pay more attention, and listen. It is a process. I am eternally grateful for the patience, grace, and teachings of my colleagues. Being in such a new place—in every meaning of that phrase—can be quite humbling, but I will tell you something I've learned from being here. It is not just political talk to say that true diversity adds more spirit and vibrancy to a community—it is Truth, or at least truth, as I believe it's intended to be.

CHAPTER 15

Consequences

RACE FOR THE CURE

Mid-June 2002 (Age 30)

In mid-June, a few weeks after I'd returned from the Caribbean, I was standing in downtown St. Louis with thousands of people, and I was trying desperately to get in touch with Jim. A sea of women wearing Talent for Senate ballcaps and Susan G. Komen Race for the Cure T-shirts was surrounding me, ready to walk in support of breast cancer research. But Jim was nowhere to be found.

Back when we first started developing the strategy for Jim's campaign, we knew that his race would likely come down in great part to the women's vote. Polling showed that men overwhelmingly supported Jim, but women felt more tentative about him, particularly in St. Louis and Kansas City. Women didn't dislike him; they just hadn't made up their mind about him—and they were skeptical. Lloyd told me it was my job to figure out ways to bring them into the fold.

Our first Women for Talent event was born in December 2001 when the Republican politician and TV personality Mary

Matalin came to St. Louis to campaign for us. Coddy had been the conduit; Mary was the very first person I asked for after President Bush. When hundreds of women packed a St. Louis ballroom to capacity to hear Mary speak over lunch, I knew we had a goldmine of an idea on our hands. We duplicated the concept around the state with different well-known women—in old theaters, converted train stations, the ballroom at the Kansas City Chiefs football complex, and the event space at the original Bass Pro Shops in Springfield. We ordered thousands of Women for Talent lapel pins and gave them out at the lunches. Every one of our events sold out within days.

We were starting to move the needle when I had the brainstorm to host a group of women to walk St. Louis's Race for the Cure in honor of Jim's mother, who had died of breast cancer. We posted a banner message on the Talent for Senate website and sent emails and postcards to Republican women across St. Louis. Over one hundred supporters had turned out to walk with us, and the race was about to start. I couldn't find Jim.

I dialed his cell number again. On the third ring, he picked up.

"Jim!" I screamed into the phone.

"Hel-lo." He cheerfully sang his greeting, and I could hear wrappers in the background. "Sorry. I had to get the kids something to eat at McDonald's."

"The race is about to start, Jim!"

"I'm coming, I promise. But remind me again where I'm supposed to park?"

I gave him directions—again—and hung up the phone. I sighed.

Every time, I said to myself. *Every single time that man drives himself to a campaign event, he gets himself into a bungle.* I rolled my eyes in exasperation.

I almost never let Jim drive himself anywhere because he

was always late, he always got lost, and these qualities brought on heart attack–like symptoms in my body every time I waited for him, like now. To counteract these issues, one of my very first campaign hires was a dapper and personable young man named Gregg Keller; he served as Jim's travel assistant. Gregg drove Jim to events all around the state and then supported him during the events. They got along terrifically well. Gregg laughed at all of Jim's jokes and could be trusted with the most sensitive pieces of information. To this day, he remains one of the best hires I've ever made. Although they presented very differently—Gregg had perfectly coiffed, highly gelled hair and wore lavender and kelly green pocket squares while Jim was understated and conservative—Gregg and Jim had similar tastes, a necessity for getting along on long car rides. But unlike Jim, Gregg was able to reliably show up on time. He also reported directly to me, which meant that he could not avoid my phone calls like Jim could.

Today, however, Gregg was barred from driving Jim. In fact, under the terms of our agreement with Missouri Right to Life, I was the only senior staffer permitted to walk in the Race for the Cure alongside Jim, and I was still fuming about it.

A week earlier, Lloyd had walked sheepishly into my office and shut the door. "Well, Jen. I got some news for you."

"What's up?"

"I just got off a call with Missouri Pro Life. They are threatening to pull their support for our campaign if we don't back out of the Race for the Cure."

"What on earth are you talking about?" I said incredulously.

"The Missouri Right to Life Committee opposes the Susan G. Komen Foundation because they give a percentage of their funding to abortion clinics."

"What percentage?"

"Like one percent."

I huffed at him. "That is ridiculous, Lloyd. Jim is one of the most pro-life candidates in America. He has a one hundred–percent rating from the National Right to Life Committee. One hundred percent!"

"Yes, Jen. But Missouri Pro Life is very powerful, and their members turn out to vote."

"What the hell are they going to do?" I scoffed. "Support Jean Carnahan? I don't think so."

"No, but they will pull support from us. Mark my words. Their lack of support would be very bad for Jim. I'm sorry, Jen. I know how hard you've been working on this."

"Screw that. We're not backing out. I already have over one hundred women signed up. You told me to get you women. Well, I'm getting you women."

"Yes, ma'am. I know that."

"And we've been publicizing this for weeks on our website."

"Yes, ma'am, I—"

"And we'll have egg all over our faces if we pull out now. *That* will be the story, Lloyd. How Jim pulled out of the race! And what do you think a media story like that will do? I'll tell you what it will do. Drive away moderate women. And another thing." I was on a roll, like a windup toy that had been wound too tightly. Lloyd watched me spin, letting me run out of steam before he reengaged. "Let's not forget *why* we're doing this. Jim's mother *died* of breast cancer, for Christ's sake!"

"Jen, I hear you. I really do. But I'm between a rock and a hard place here. Let me call them back and see what I can do."

He came back into my office a few hours later, telling me he'd brokered a compromise.

"Okay. Here's the deal. You can still walk, but only you and

Jim can be involved. We need to stop promoting the race on our website, and there can be no more emails about it."

I looked at him without saying anything. His stare communicated that this was his best and final offer.

"Capisce?" he asked while staring me down. He expected an answer, and I didn't want to give him one.

"Funny," I said, "how making deals with conservative Christian groups is like making deals with the devil." As I said this, it occurred to me how many such deals with the devil I'd made in my hyper-religious lifetime.

I could tell by Lloyd's pained expression that he did not like my saying this. He raised his voice in exasperation.

"*Capisce?!*"

"Capisce," I said, full of disdain but relieved we didn't have to cancel.

On the day of the event, Jim arrived at our gathering spot a full thirty seconds before the race began. Wearing his Talent for Senate ballcap and Race for the Cure T-shirt, just like I'd asked him to, he had Michael, Kate, and Chrissy in tow. They all looked so energized and excited that I instantly forgave him.

"Welcome to the party, Congressman Talent," I said, while rolling my eyes in jest.

"Good to be here, counselor," he said with a twinkle in his eye.

For the next few hours, we walked the 5K loop around downtown St. Louis while chatting with supporters and friends. As I walked, I didn't think too much about my own muddled feelings about abortion. Should it really be banned for everyone no matter what, like Jim believed? That seemed harsh, but I didn't want to be one of those waffling, spineless, pro-choice Republicans, either. I figured it was best not to think about it too much; it wasn't as if there was a possibility abortion would be illegal again, so why rock the boat? I preferred to congratulate myself for holding the line on walking the Race for the Cure . . . or at least sort of holding the line. It was far more convenient to simply ignore the whole issue—to go along in order to get along—than to stir up any additional inner conflict for myself. I'd already had more than enough conflict to deal with on the campaign, thank you very much.

KCTV CHANNEL 5

June 24, 2022 (Age 49)

I stumbled across a news article in June 2022, immediately after the United States Supreme Court overturned *Roe vs. Wade*:

> KANSAS CITY, Mo (KCTV)—Missouri Attorney General Eric Schmitt released a statement Friday morning that the Show-Me State was the first in the country to "effectively end abortion."

The attorney general signed an opinion minutes after the Supreme Court of the United States ruling that Roe v. Wade had been overturned.

"This is a monumental day for the sanctity of life," Schmitt tweeted.

House Bill 126 passed in the Missouri General Assembly in 2019 was signed to trigger a ban on abortions in the state once SCOTUS overturned Roe v. Wade, and then after Missouri's governor or attorney general certified it.

Parson and Schmitt did just that Friday morning, making abortions illegal in the state of Missouri.

BABIES

June 2008 (Age 36)

Six years after the campaign ended, and six months after giving birth to my first child, my son Jack, I had an abortion. I have never written that down before; I've never even said it out loud. For a very long time, even the word *abortion* toxically insinuated to me a horrible woman who is the most selfish and irresponsible person on the planet, and probably a crack addict besides. I hated the word *abortion* so much it hurts me to write it, and what I mean by this is that I feel a literal ache in that place inside my body that my therapist is teaching me to pay attention to. But I've written it here because it's true. I had an abortion.

Now, sixteen years later, I can say without any reservations that I would do the exact same thing again, and I support every other woman who has to make a similar choice, no matter the circumstances. I say this with all my might and soul and strength. But many years ago, this was far from the case.

After I had spent a year and a half trying to get pregnant, my OBGYN sent me in for testing. It took a few weeks for an endocrinologist to diagnose the problem. I had polycystic ovary syndrome, or PCOS, a condition most common in obese and diabetic women. Given that I was a size 4 and in perfect health, the diagnosis was a shock. I was sent home with a prescription for metformin, and it took two weeks to jump-start my ovulation. I got pregnant, and nine months later, my healthy Jack was born in December 2007.

Women with PCOS often have difficulties breastfeeding, so I stayed on the metformin. By early spring, however, I realized I had not gotten my period in a long time, and, on a whim, I took a pregnancy test. Jack was only five months old, and I was pregnant again. I called my OBGYN, and they booked my twelve-week appointment.

Leading up to my appointment, I realized how different my body felt this time around. I had horrible morning sickness—something I'd never experienced with Jack—and I felt nauseous all the time. I kept a large stainless steel bowl next to my bed, which I heaved into frequently.

I wonder if I'm having a girl, I thought.

At my twelve-week appointment (which, I came to find out, landed closer to my seventeenth week of pregnancy), I was escorted into the ultrasound room. I lay flat on the table, and the technician put that cold, gooey jelly on my bare stomach. She took out her monitor and began sliding it all over my belly. With Jack, the technician had talked while she did this, saying things like "The baby looks healthy!" and "There are the arms!" But this technician sat in silence for a few moments before excusing herself from the room, saying she needed to get my doctor.

Clearly, something was wrong. When my doctor came in, she moved the ultrasound monitor around my stomach. The screen in front of me was turned off.

"How are you feeling, Jen?"

"Well, I'm tired all the time, like when I was pregnant with Jack. But I have terrible nausea and morning sickness. Am I having a girl?" I said this with great hope, praying I'd misread the situation.

"You are pregnant with a girl, yes," she said. "But, Jen, there is a problem."

I was then told that our unborn daughter had no arms and legs, and her heart was not forming properly. She would likely die within the next month.

"When that happens," my doctor explained calmly, "your life, Jen, *your* life will be at serious risk."

A rush of guilt overtook me. Were my baby's health issues my fault? I pummeled my doctor with questions. Could it have been that I overexerted myself while caring for Jack because I didn't know I was pregnant? Could I have contracted some illness while traveling to Central America for two weeks? I'd had two glasses of wine a few nights before I knew I was pregnant—could that be it? At thirty-six, was I too old to have another baby?

"No," she said emphatically. "No. Nothing you did caused this to happen." But I didn't believe her.

On the day of the procedure, I felt numb. I remember very little other than sitting in a strange room waiting for it to happen. I cried all the way home. My overwhelming sense of loss and failure blinded me to the point where I thought I would never recover, and I mourned the loss with every sinew of my being. She is with me, still.

CHAPTER 16

Love

WHAT I KNOW TO BE TRUE

September 2023 (Age 52)

At the intersection of Fifth Street and Dearborn, I stopped walking and looked up. Above the mountains and palm trees was a sunset so beautiful it looked like a painting. Deep magenta, bright pink, and red patches outlined by navy blue zigzags lit up the sky, like preschool artwork that had been made with the entire box of crayons. The mountains below shimmered as if illuminated by fire, and the seventy-foot-tall California palm trees swayed gracefully in the light breeze. I struggled to take in so much beauty all at once.

The late Irish poet John O'Donohue has said that our lives are changed by living in a place where the landscape around us feels as alive as we are. I have been to some of the world's most stunning spots, but the wilds of California feel more alive to me than anywhere else does. Something about the dry desert earth and the life that emerges from its barrenness shatters me, and nowhere else have I seen palm trees frame snow-covered mountains like they do here. Then there are the sunsets, for which I have found no words.

From my sidewalk spot at Fifth and Dearborn, the sun began sinking faster and then dipped behind the mountains. The colors of the fluorescent sky darkened, and the city lights twinkled in the valley below. Cars raced down Fifth Street, oblivious to the magic unfolding in the sky. *Look up, look up!* I wanted to shout. *You are missing the whole thing!*

What is it that finally gets our attention, reminding us to look up? I do not know. But it always happens at the very moment it is needed, even if, at the time, it feels too late.

SONGS

1984 (Age 13)

When I was thirteen years old, I auditioned to train as an opera singer at the Interlochen Center for the Arts in Interlochen, Michigan.

I'd been taking voice lessons for a few years, and the movie *Amadeus*, starring F. Murray Abraham and Tom Hulce, had just come out. I loved that movie, and Tom Hulce was an Interlochen graduate. It had only been a couple of years since my dad and I had The Talk in his office and wrote down my goals. *I want to be a singer*, I'd said to him. And now here I was, ready to sing.

As my mom's Volvo drove onto the campus, I sat in the front passenger seat, absolutely terrified. She'd pulled into a parking space, and in front of me was Interlochen's renowned outdoor amphitheater, where some of the most famous musicians in the world had performed. With its four thousand seats, it was an exquisite building nestled on the shoreline of Green Lake. This was the audition venue, and I was no less scared than I would have been if I was performing at the Met.

I sat trembling in the car. I wouldn't, *couldn't*, get out of my seat. Girls who looked like *Vogue* cover models walked by my window, giggling. They were dressed in black with high-heeled boots and gold jewelry. They flipped their long, perfect blonde hair, which fell like strands of gold over their shoulders. They didn't look nervous; to them, this was just another day. I could hear people in the distance singing scales to warm up.

I looked at myself in the rearview mirror. My hair was permed, short and brown; I wore no makeup, and my blue dress hugged me around the neck. It was my mom's suggestion, and I felt like a schoolgirl among the glitterati.

"You'll be fine," my mom said. "Because you *are* fine. *You are you.*"

"I have no business being here," I said. "Let's go. I don't want to do this anymore."

"Yes," she said, placing her hand gently on mine. "You *do* want to be here. You have practiced for months. No one can make you who you are. Only you can show them that."

I opened the car door and walked slowly down the pathway to the amphitheater. Tall oaks and sugar maples stretched high into the sky, their leaves rustling in the wind. In a few short weeks, I'd be heading back to summer camp, and this place reminded me of the peace and joy I felt there. The rustling leaves also reminded me to pray. Silently, I told myself that God was here, and under these trees, I felt God. I repeated the lines of Psalm 91, which I knew by heart:

> *He that dwelleth in the secret place of the most High shall abide under the shadow of the Almighty.*
>
> *I will say of the Lord, He is my refuge and my fortress: my God; in him will I trust.*

For good measure, and maybe some good luck, I said it again. I sometimes wondered why prayer helped me, or helped anyone, really, but I wasn't thinking about that then. It was my mom who had always provided me with a satisfying answer. "God just is," she'd say. "We can't ask God to do more than he's already done. But we can avail ourselves of divine love by praying."

The stage was elevated six feet from the ground, and four thousand empty seats stretched below. I looked down, and only five front seats were occupied. The faces were severe, and they looked at clipboards while taking notes. I drew in a breath, and then I let it out. *I can do this*, I thought. And just like I always did in times of stress and fear, I steadied myself. I wanted this more than anything.

I was waiting in the wings for my name to be called, and I knew there was only one person in line to audition before it would be my turn. She was in front of me. When her name was called, she walked out to the microphone, the *click-click-click* of her heels reverberating on the Interlochen stage. I stared at an *Amadeus* movie poster that showed Tom Hulce with his white wig and wild, crazy smile.

When it was time for the girl in front of me to sing, I peeped around the curtains and watched. She opened her mouth, and a sound came out that was so beautiful I almost started to cry. I'd never heard the song before, and I'd learn later that it was called "Ave Maria." Even though the words were in Latin, it was the most magical song I'd ever heard. She shifted in her heels as she belted her voice into the microphone. She was nervous, too, and she missed a few notes. But the sound reverberated into the amphitheater like a dream. I felt like I was in a cathedral.

When she finished, she stopped and stood very still, and I had to hold back my applause. No one else applauded either. From my spot behind the curtain, I saw the five people in the front row nod and thank her. They looked down into their laps and took notes on the clipboards.

"Jen Sappenfield," I heard my name called out over the speakers, and I wanted to run. I stood in place, not moving.

"It's your turn," someone backstage whispered to me, pushing my back. I didn't move and stood completely still.

"Jen Sappenfield?" the voice said again. I took a deep breath and slowly walked onto the stage, my eyes pinned on the microphone ahead of me. My body was now in full view, all alone on that giant stage, and my girlish blue dress tugged at my neck.

A woman, one of the five people in the front row, said to me, "So what are you going to be singing for us today?"

I stood at the microphone and couldn't speak.

"Jen?" she said again.

I thought of The Monster, who was telling me I could not do this and should run back to the car. But something inside of me, a small, still voice, told me I could. Suddenly, I felt very calm.

"Yes, hello, I'm Jen," I said, my voice squeaking into the mic. I put my right hand on the microphone stand to adjust the height.

The five figures below me nodded, relieved. They sat back more comfortably in their chairs.

"I'm going to be singing 'Country Roads' by John Denver," I told them. "It's one of my dad's favorite songs, and mine, too."

I could tell from the faces of the five people in front of me that they were about to laugh. "Country Roads" is no "Ave Maria."

But then I began to sing. I sang the song as I had practiced it a million times and got lost in the sound of my own voice. I felt like I was the Voice of God, with no awareness of the amphitheater, any other girl auditioning, or the five people in the front row. When I finished, I came back to my own body, and it took me a minute to remember where I was. That's when my eyes shifted down to the front row. The five teachers said nothing while they wrote on sheets of paper. Finally, they thanked me, and another name was called. I walked back to my place behind the curtain.

"How did it go?" my mom asked me when I returned to the car.

"I'm not sure," I replied. "But I did it. And I did the best I could."

A month later, a letter from the Interlochen Center for the Arts told me that I'd gotten in.

I read the letter ten times to make sure, and then I read it to my mom and dad.

My mom whirled me around the kitchen. My dad was focused on the next steps.

"You have been working hard. I'm glad we mapped out your goals so you had clarity on what you needed to do."

I've thought about that day more times than I can count over the past forty years. In 2022, when I was sitting in my psychotherapist's office, I told her about it. *What a clinical response,* I thought as I talked. *Didn't he even care?*

"Is that all you remember from that day?" Nichoel said quietly.

I sat and thought for a long time. I searched backward into my memories until I remembered something, and I jumped a little in my seat.

"Actually, no," I responded with great surprise.

"No?" Nichoel asked, raising an eyebrow. "What else do you remember?"

I paused for what felt like an inordinately long time. I was looking at Nichoel, and she was looking at me.

I stumbled over my words. "I think . . . I think . . . my dad said he was proud of me. I think he said, 'Very well done.'"

Nichoel watched me intently as she said her next words. "Do you believe what he said?"

I felt what I was going to say next, in that place inside my body where I know things.

"Yes, Nichoel. I do."

THRESHOLDS

March 2024 (Age 52)

I was lying face down on John's massage table with my face wedged in the hole of the terrycloth ring at the top. John was pressing on my back as hard as he could, coming at his treatment for the ongoing pain in my ribs in a new way.

"Breathe, Jen."

I took a large breath and slowly released it. Then he said it again.

"Breathe again."

I obeyed.

"And again."

With each breath, he would push down on my spine so hard I thought my spine and ribs would crack—either that or I would buckle from the pain. He felt me struggling and told me to stop resisting.

"Relax into the pain," he said. I kept my focus on breathing.

Within moments, my mind began floating into nothingness, a half-awake, half-asleep dream state. I could feel the pain in my body at the very same time I felt its release. This was the paradox that came with seeing John—and, I suppose, with life. That was when I heard the inside-me/outside-me disembodied Voice. It was the first time I'd heard it since being on the clipper ship in the Caribbean twenty-two years before.

In the quiet of John's studio, the Voice said, "Your only job is to love." The words hung in the space around me like air.

When I heard it, I did not jump or gasp like I had two decades earlier. I was older now, and the older Jen knew that God uses many ways to communicate. Our job is to listen.

Love how? I silently asked. *And love who?*

"Just love." It was the last thing the Voice said to me.

John touched my shoulder lightly.

"Done," he whispered. "I think we finally got everything out of those ribs. They won't be bothering you so much anymore."

To which I replied, "You know, I think you are right."

It took me a while to find my clothes and then regain my balance while putting on underpants, jeans, shoes. Being in John's massage room always felt like an out-of-body experience, and opening the door and emerging into his bright lobby did my head in every time. As I turned the handle, I felt like I was crossing a threshold. But that's how it was with John.

My life, I realized, was a series of thresholds—times when, once I crossed over into new territory, I could not turn back.

When I crossed the Continental Divide on my drive from Virginia to California to start my new university job in late 2020, the sun was just rising, and a light dusting of snow shimmered on the highway. It was early November, and I was one hundred miles west of Albuquerque. Very few other vehicles were on the road. The sign on Highway 40 marked the spot with the words *Continental Divide*, and below that was a note saying that from this point forward, rainfall to the east would flow into the Atlantic Ocean; to the west, into the Pacific. The invisible line seemed almost mystical, like one of the universe's thin spaces where the divine feels most easily accessible. As I crossed over, it was so quiet I could hear the whir of my car's tires on the road. I knew that this journey, like all journeys, was every bit as important as the destination.

I also knew I could never go back.

BUTTERFLY

June 2024 (Age 52)

My university office is the size of a glorified closet. The space had originally served as the men's bathroom before becoming an office, but you have to know where to look to find evidence of that. The urinal plumbing is hidden behind my credenza, and drywall expertly covers the pipes. I've tucked a love seat and small chairs at one end and my desk at the other. A few carefully placed lamps soften the lighting. Two large Mark Rothko prints hang next to mementos from my congressional days. The smallest and most quirky office I've had in my long career, it is also my favorite.

But the best thing about my office is the view from my window onto the university quad, with a lawn so impossibly green it takes my breath away. On many afternoons, I put my feet up on my desk, cross my legs, and look outside at the beauty of the landscape. This is what I'm doing now, and I am thinking about the woman I am becoming. When I look back at my life, it almost feels as if I'm watching a movie where my character falls down in scene after scene, often tragically. She makes me so sad that I sometimes want to cry. I know her sorrow and her loneliness deeply, of course, and she breaks my heart.

The person I'd constructed myself to be when I was young has been literally knocked out of me, and as I move further away from her, I have come back to center and found myself—my real self. This process took what felt like an impossibly long time. I had to develop a completely new understanding of what belonging meant, along with a new way to belong. I can still feel the anguish of those years pulsing inside my chest. But the sensation is different now than it used to be. I no longer feel a racing panic; instead, there's a knowing that I survived—that I *can* survive. I feel safe inside those memories now. I am filled with so much forgiveness and empathy that I am often inspired to cheer my younger self on. *You're going to make it, Jen. Hang on, Jen. You can do it.* It is like Present-Day Jen has finally joined with Past Jen, and when I think about her, she is so beautiful that I don't just *want* to cry, I actually do.

I recently read a blog post by Paulo Coelho, Brazilian author of *The Alchemist*, which, coincidentally, is one of my very favorite books. He wrote the post years ago, on December 10, 2007, the same day that my oldest son, Jack, was born. It tells the story of a man who takes pity on a butterfly struggling to emerge from its cocoon. The man sits for hours watching the butterfly push and pull to get out, seemingly unable to escape. The struggle bothers him so much that he uses a pair of scissors to release it. A few moments later, the butterfly dies. Nature requires the butterfly to struggle so it strengthens its wings, Coelho's post said, which can be almost impossible to watch. But when the butterfly flutters its wings at last, there is nothing on earth more magnificent.

I am reminded of this story now as I look down at the university quad. The green grass stretches in front of me, and the brilliant blue of the sky frames the university chapel at the other end. In the stillness, it occurs to me that meaning can only come by way of wholeness, and wholeness, it must be said, does not come easily. When we have been broken and the pieces finally come together, only then can we begin to understand the complexity of a meaningful life. When our soul stirs, that is when we become who we are meant to be. It is the only way we can finally know what joy is, and the depths that must be mined before we feel free.

For my own part, I remain chasing the boar.

Acknowledgments

In her poem "The World I Live In," Mary Oliver writes that only if there are angels in our head can we ever possibly see one. I have been surrounded by angels for the past twenty years as this book—and its author—have come to life. My gratitude for them knows no bounds.

To Brooke Warner and Shannon Green at She Writes Press, Signe Jorgensen, and the Simon & Schuster team, my deepest thanks for taking such thoughtful care of my vision and manuscript, and for shepherding this book into being.

There would be no book without Parker J. Palmer, the brilliant author, activist, and poet, who believed in my work and me since we were first connected. My gratitude for his support is profound.

To my beloved mother and brother who have been there for me every step of the way: Thank you for loving me like you do.

I hit the jackpot with my friends. Jenny Rand Smith, my cauldron sister since I was fourteen years old, has walked with me on this path longer than anyone, believing in me and my vision for this book from the beginning. Shelli Stockton held my hand and spent countless hours reading every word I've written to help me refine and stay true to myself. My JESS, Stephanie Johnson and Ericka Smith—you are golden to me. Adam

Johnson, thank you for so masterfully designing my website. Larry and Char Burgess, my guides and mentor-friends, care for me like siblings. Todd Loza, so much love and thank you for making me look (and feel) good. Paul, thank you for your partnership. And to Jim and Deb Fallows, my beloved Devon Parsons, Chris Spear, and Ann Bryan, thank you.

I have had great fortune to have the best bosses. Krista Newkirk and Jim Ashby, thank you for inspiring me with your leadership and supporting me—I am endlessly grateful. Bob Lindgren, you taught me so much about digging in and finding meaning, and I admire you greatly. Bob Holsworth, you are a force of brilliance and grace. Senator Jim Talent, thank you, thank you—you were my role model and my family, and I am honored to have been by your side for all those years.

To my spiritual, health, and writing mentors and guides—you stuck with me no matter what to help me see and understand. Nichoel Kimmerle, you are the best therapist on the planet—hands down. John Webster, you brought my body back to life with insight and care. Reverend Gary Jones, I do not have the words for all that you taught and modeled for me. Curtis Almquist, I am endlessly grateful for your spiritual might and for your laughter. Shari Caudron, the memoir whisperer, you helped me find my voice again when I wasn't sure I could use it anymore. Tim Myers, thank you for lifting me up and for seeing me in the very best way.

And to my sons, Jack and Michael, to whom this book is dedicated, I love you beyond anything in this world.

About the Author

Photo credit: Coco McKown

Jen Thompson is a former political campaign manager and counsel in the US House and Senate. She successfully made up for a massive campaign deficit by orchestrating events with the President of the United States and other key figures. She has been quoted in *The New York Times, The Washington Post, The Chicago Tribune*, and others. Jen left politics after managing the most nationally watched Senate campaign in 2002 and moved to Australia. Born in Chicago, Jen has lived in twelve cities, seven states, and three countries, and has traveled to many more. She currently lives in Redlands, California.